15 Days of Prayer
With Saint Thérèse of Lisieux

Also in this collection:

André Dupleix
15 Days of Prayer
With Teilhard de Chardin

André Gozier
15 Days of Prayer
With Thomas Merton

Michel Lafon
15 Days of Prayer
With Charles de Foucauld

François Vayne
15 Days of Prayer
With Saint Bernadette of Lourdes

15 DAYS OF PRAYER

WITH

Saint Thérèse of Lisieux

CONSTANT TONNELIER

Translated by Victoria Hébert and Denis Sabourin

Liguori
LIGUORI, MISSOURI

Published by Liguori Publications
Liguori, Missouri
http://www.liguori.org

This book is a translation of *Prier 15 Jours Avec Thérèse de Lisieux*
published by Nouvelle Cité, 1996, Montrouge, France.

English translation copyright 1999 by Liguori Publications

Library of Congress Cataloging-in-Publication Data

Tonnelier, Constant
    [Prier 15 jours avec Thérèse of Lisieux. English]
    15 days of prayer with Saint Thérèse of Lisieux / Constant Tonnelier ;
translated by Victoria Hébert and Denis Sabourin. — 1st English ed.
    p. cm.
    Includes bibliographical references.
    ISBN 0-7648-0492-8 (pbk.)
    1. Thérèse, de Lisieux, Saint, 1873–1897 Prayer-books and devo-
tions—English. I. Thérèse, de Lisieux, Saint 1873–1897. II. Title. III.
Title: Fifteen days of prayer with Saint Thérèse of Lisieux.
    BX2179.T53T6613 1999
    269'.6—dc21   99–26794

Printed in the United States of America
03 02 01 00 99   5 4 3 2 1
First English Edition 1999

Table of Contents

How to Use This Book

AN OLD CHINESE PROVERB, or at least what I am able to recall of what is supposed to be an old Chinese proverb, goes something like this: "Even a journey of a thousand miles begins with a single step." When you think about it, the truth of the proverb is obvious. It is impossible to begin any project, let alone a journey, without taking the first step. I think it might also be true, although I cannot recall if another Chinese proverb says it, "that the first step is often the hardest." Or, as someone else once observed, "the distance between a thought and the corresponding action needed to implement the idea takes the most energy." I don't know who shared that perception with me but I am certain it was not an old Chinese master!

With this ancient proverbial wisdom, and the not-so-ancient wisdom of an unknown contemporary sage still fresh, we move from proverbs to presumptions. How do these relate to the task before us?

I am presuming that if you are reading this introduction it is because you are contemplating a journey. My presumption is that you are preparing for a spiritual journey and that you have taken at least some of the first steps necessary to prepare for this journey. I also presume, and please excuse me if I am making too many presumptions, that in your preparation for the spiritual journey you have determined that you need a guide. From deep within the recesses of your deepest self, there was something that called you to consider Thérèse of Lisieux as a potential companion. If my presumptions are correct, may I congratulate you on this decision? I think you have made a wise choice, a choice that can be confirmed by yet another source of wisdom, the wisdom that comes from practical experience.

Even an informal poll of experienced travelers will reveal a common opinion; it is very difficult to travel alone. Some might observe that it is even foolish. Still others may be even stronger in their opinion and go so far as to insist that it is necessary to have a guide, especially when you are traveling into uncharted waters and into territory that you have not yet experienced. I am of the personal opinion that a traveling companion is welcome under all circumstances. The thought of traveling alone, to some exciting destination without someone to share the journey with does not capture my imagination or channel my enthusiasm. However, with that being noted, what is simply a matter of preference on the normal journey becomes a matter of necessity when a person embarks on a spiritual journey.

The spiritual journey, which can be the most challenging of all journeys, is experienced best with a guide, a companion, or at the very least, a friend in whom you have placed your trust. This observation is not a preference or an opinion but rather an established spiritual necessity. All of the great saints with whom I am familiar had a spiritual director or a confessor who journeyed with them. Admittedly, at times the saint might well have traveled far beyond the experience of their guide and companion but more often than not they would return to their director and reflect on their experience.

Understood in this sense, the director and companion provided a valuable contribution and necessary resource.

When I was learning how to pray (a necessity for anyone who desires to be a full-time and public "religious person"), the community of men that I belong to gave me a great gift. Between my second and third year in college, I was given a one-year sabbatical, with all expenses paid and all of my personal needs met. This period of time was called novitiate. I was officially designated as a novice, a beginner in the spiritual journey, and I was assigned a "master," a person who was willing to lead me. In addition to the master, I was provided with every imaginable book and any other resource that I could possibly need. Even with all that I was provided, I did not learn how to pray because of the books and the unlimited resources, rather it was the master, the companion who was the key to the experience.

One day, after about three months of reading, of quiet and solitude, and of practicing all of the methods and descriptions of prayer that were available to me, the master called. "Put away the books, forget the method, and just listen." We went into a room, became quiet, and tried to recall the presence of God, and then, the master simply prayed out loud and permitted me to listen to his prayer. As he prayed, he revealed his hopes, his dreams, his struggles, his successes, and most of all, his relationship with God. I discovered as I listened that his prayer was deeply intimate but most of all it was self-revealing. As I learned about him, I was led through his life experience to the place where God dwells. At that moment I was able to understand a little bit about what I was supposed to do if I really wanted to pray.

The dynamic of what happened when the master called, invited me to listen, and then revealed his innermost self to me as he communicated with God in prayer, was important. It wasn't so much that the master was trying to reveal to me what needed to be said; he was not inviting me to pray with the same words that he used, but rather that he was trying to bring me to that place within myself where prayer becomes possible. That place, a place of intimacy and of self-awareness, was a necessary stop on the journey and it was a place that I needed to be led to. I could not have easily discovered it on my own.

The purpose of the volume that you hold in your hand is to lead you, over a period of fifteen days or, maybe more realistically, fifteen prayer periods, to a place where prayer is possible. If you already have a regular experience and practice of prayer, perhaps this volume can help lead you to a deeper place, a more intimate relationship with the Lord.

It is important to note that the purpose of this book is not to lead you to a better relationship with Thérèse of Lisieux, your spiritual companion. Although your companion will invite you to share some of their deepest and most intimate thoughts, your companion is doing so only to bring you to that place where God dwells. After all, the true measurement of a companion for the journey is that they bring you to the place where you need to be, and then they step back, out of the picture. A guide who brings you to the desired destination and then sticks around is a very unwelcome guest!

Many times I have found myself attracted to a particular idea or method for accomplishing a task, only to discover that what seemed to be inviting and helpful possessed too many details. All of my energy went to the mastery of the details and I soon lost my enthusiasm. In each instance, the book that seemed so promising ended up on my bookshelf, gathering dust. I can assure you, it is not our intention that this book end up in your bookcase, filled with promise, but unable to deliver.

There are three simple rules that need to be followed in order to use this book with a measure of satisfaction.

Place: It is important that you choose a place for reading that provides the necessary atmosphere for reflection and that does not allow for too many distractions. Whatever place you choose needs to be comfortable, have the necessary lighting, and, finally, have a sense of "welcoming" about it. You need to be able to look forward to the experience of the journey. Don't travel steerage if you know you will be more comfortable in first class and if the choice is realistic for you. On the other hand, if first class is a distraction and you feel more comfortable and more yourself in steerage, then it is in steerage that you belong.

My favorite place is an overstuffed and comfortable chair in my bedroom. There is a light over my shoulder, and the chair reclines if I feel a need to recline. Once in a while, I get lucky and the sun comes through my window and bathes the entire room in light. I have other options and other places that are available to me but this is the place that I prefer.

Time: Choose a time during the day when you are most alert and when you are most receptive to reflection, meditation, and prayer. The time that you choose is an essential component. If you are a morning person, for example, you should choose a time that is in the morning. If you are more alert in the afternoon, choose an afternoon time slot; and if evening is your preference, then by all means choose the evening. Try to avoid "peak" periods in your daily routine when you know that you might be disturbed. The time that you choose needs to be your time and needs to work for you.

It is also important that you choose how much time you will spend with your companion each day. For some it will be possible to set aside enough time in order to read and reflect on all the material that is offered for a given day. For others, it might not be possible to devote one time to the suggested material for the day, so the prayer period may need to be extended for two, three, or even more sessions. It is not important how long it takes you; it is only important that it works for you and that you remain committed to that which is possible.

For myself I have found that fifteen minutes in the early morning, while I am still in my robe and pajamas and before my morning coffee, and even before I prepare myself for the day, is the best time. No one expects to see me or to interact with me because I have not yet "announced" the fact that I am awake or even on the move. However, once someone hears me in the bathroom, then my window of opportunity is gone. It is therefore important to me that I use the time that I have identified when it is available to me.

Freedom: It may seem strange to suggest that freedom is the third necessary ingredient, but I have discovered that it is most important. By freedom I understand a certain "stance toward life," a "permission to be myself and to be gentle and understanding of who I am." I am constantly amazed at how the human person so easily sets himself or herself up for disappointment and perceived failure. We so easily make judgments about ourselves and our actions and our choices, and very often those judgments are negative, and not at all helpful.

For instance, what does it really matter if I have chosen a place and a time, and I have missed both the place and the time for three days in a row? What does it matter if I have chosen, in that twilight time before I am completely awake and still a little sleepy, to roll over and to sleep for fifteen minutes more? Does it mean that I am not serious about the journey, that I really don't want to pray, that I am just fooling myself when I say that my prayer time is important to me? Perhaps, but I prefer to believe that it simply means that I am tired and I just wanted a little more sleep. It doesn't mean anything more than that. However, if I make it mean more than that, then I can become discouraged, frustrated, and put myself into a state where I might more easily give up. "What's the use? I might as well forget all about it."

The same sense of freedom applies to the reading and the praying of this text. If I do not find the introduction to each day helpful, I don't need to read it. If I find the questions for reflection at the end of the appointed day repetitive, then I should choose to close the book and go my own way. Even if I discover that the reflection offered for the day is not the one that I prefer and that the one for the next day seems more inviting, then by all means, go on to the one for the next day.

That's it! If you apply these simple rules to your journey you should receive the maximum benefit and you will soon find yourself at your destination. But be prepared to be surprised. If you have never been on a spiritual journey you should know that the "travel brochures" and the other descriptions that you might have heard are nothing compared to the real thing. There is so much more than you can imagine.

A final prayer of blessing suggests itself:

> Lord, catch me off guard today.
> Surprise me with some moment of beauty
>   or pain
> So that at least for the moment
> I may be startled into seeing that you are
>   here in all your splendor,
> Always and everywhere,
> Barely hidden,
> Beneath,
> Beyond,
> Within this life I breathe.
>
> —*Frederick Buechner*

REV. THOMAS M. SANTA, CSsR
LIGUORI, MISSOURI
FEAST OF THE PRESENTATION, 1999

A Chronology of the Life
of Saint Thérèse of Lisieux

1873: Born to Louis Martin, a watchmaker, and Zélie-Marie Martin, a lacemaker, at Alençon, France. Youngest of five children.

1876: Thérèse's mother dies of breast cancer; the Martin family move to Lisieux.

1879: Thérèse makes her first Confession at St. Peter's Cathedral.

1882: Thérèse's elder sister Pauline enters the Carmelite Convent of Lisieux.

1884: Thérèse makes her first Communion and is confirmed.

1886: Thérèse's sister Marie leaves to join the Carmelites of Lisieux. Thérèse is subject to constant tearful episodes and prays for a miracle to overcome them. Her prayers are granted.

1887: Thérèse tells her father that she too wishes to join the Carmelites. Thérèse asks permission of the bishop of Bayeux to enter the Carmelites. After a visit to Rome and an audience with the pope, Thérèse receives permission to enter the Carmelites at Easter of the following year.

1888: On the feast of the Annunciation, aged fifteen years and four months, Thérèse enters the Carmelite convent of Lisieux as a postulant.

1889: Thérèse is formally clothed as a nun and is now Sister Thérèse of the Child Jesus and the Holy Face.

1890: Thérèse makes her Profession on the feast of Our Lady's Nativity and, several weeks later, takes the veil.

1891: Thérèse becomes assistant sacristan.

1893: Thérèse's elder sister Pauline (Sister Agnes of Jesus) is elected prioress of the Lisieux convent. Later, in the Spring, she is appointed assistant mistress of novices.

1894: Louis Martin, Thérèse's father dies in July; in September, Thérèse's sister Céline enters the Carmelite convent and becomes Sister Geneviève of the Holy Face and of Saint Thérèse.

1896: Thérèse finishes writing her autobiography, *The Story of a Soul,* and gives it to the prioress, who had ordered her to write her memoirs. Later that year, Thérèse begins coughing up blood and experiences her own bout of spiritual depression.

1897: Thérèse becomes seriously ill in April; in July she is taken to the convent infirmary and receives the last sacraments. On September 30, after much suffering, Thérèse dies, surrounded by the community. Her last words are "My God, I love you."

1923: Thérèse is beatified by Pope Pius XI.

1925: Thérèse of the Child Jesus is canonized by Pope Pius XI. Her feast day is October 3.

1927: Pope Pius XI names Thérèse Patroness of all Missionaries, together with Saint Francis Xavier.

1980: Pope John Paul II makes a pilgrimage to Lisieux.

1998: Pope John Paul II proclaims Saint Thérèse of Lisieux a Doctor of the Church.

A Few Notes About Saint Thérèse of Lisieux

ON SEPTEMBER 30, 1897, around 7:20 in the evening, Thérèse left her beloved Carmel and her home in Lisieux, transported by love: "I am not dying," she said, "I am beginning life." She was only twenty-four years old.

Who, then, is this little Norman who continues to shine on the world? Marie Françoise Thérèse Martin was born on January 2, 1873, in Alençon, in the Normandy region of France. She was the last of nine children born to Louis Martin and Zélie Guérin, a jeweler-watchmaker and a skilled lacemaker, respectively. A baby of frail health, she was baptized on Saturday, January 4, at Our Lady of Alençon Church. Only four of her siblings survived their childhood.

On August 28, 1877, her mother died and Thérèse became very close to her sister Pauline. Also in that same year, her family moved to Lisieux, in the Buissonnets region. On October 2, 1882, Pauline entered into religious life with the Carmelites. This was a calling that Thérèse also wished to follow. On the day of Pauline's profession, Thérèse made her first Communion on May 8, 1884, and her Confirmation shortly afterwards on June 14, 1884. Another sister, Marie, entered Carmel on October 15, 1886.

The holiness of Christmas that year especially affected Thérèse, giving her "the grace of conversion" and the grace to leave her childhood behind. It was said that she was transformed. Thérèse describes it in this way:

> In this brilliant night which illuminates the joy of the Holy Trinity, Jesus, the gentle little Child of the hour...made me strong and brave. He armed me with his weapons and, since that blessed night, I have not been defeated in any battle. To the contrary, I went from one victory to the next, to begin, more or less, "an invincible quest."
>
> *Thérèse of Lisieux, Ms A, 44v–45r*

Little Thérèse had found the strength of soul, and she would always seek to preserve it.

Thérèse's fondest wish was to enter the Carmelite order, but she was only fifteen years of age. She made a personal plea to Rome, all the way to Pope Leo XIII, to receive special dispensation, but the outcome of her pilgrimage still left her in limbo and unsure of receiving the required permission. All hope seemed lost, but the bishop of Bayeux did grant the required permission a few days after Christmas in 1887. On April 9, 1888, during the Easter season, on the feast of the Annunciation, her dream became a reality; she entered the Carmelites in Lisieux. She was fifteen years and four months old! An astonishing feat, even if thought of in today's terms.

Before her rose could bloom, Thérèse had to suffer the pricks of thorns. Even though her two sisters were with her, Thérèse respected the rigors of monastic life. She suffered greatly at the death of her father. Her letters to her sister

Céline showed just how much she was affected. After having experienced a period of barren faith, Thérèse professed her vows on September 8, 1890, on the feast day of the Birth of the Blessed Virgin Mary.

Four years later the symptoms of the illness which would eventually take her life began to appear. After suffering such deep sorrow at the death of her father on July 29, 1894, a profound happiness came to her as her sister Céline also entered the Carmelites on September 14, 1894, on the feast day of the Triumph of the Cross.

Thérèse's road was a road of suffering, smallness, spiritual childhood, abandonment to the benevolent love of the Lord, trials of faith, periods of painful spiritual barrenness, and a life devoted entirely to love and to the Church. Her Carmelite life spanned nine years—and echoed far beyond those simple walls in Lisieux.

Marie Martin, known as Sister Mary of the Sacred Heart, was well inspired to insist on the gathering of Thérèse's childhood memories and to obtain her secrets about her doctrine and her little way.

Pauline Martin, known as Mother Agnes of Jesus, and who was then superior of Carmel, ordered Sister Thérèse of the Child Jesus and of the Holy Face to record her childhood memories. At the age of twenty-two, in 1895, Thérèse wrote and edited a document known as Manuscript A and, with a spontaneous heart, offered it up to the benevolent love of the Lord.

The illness which was afflicting Thérèse manifested itself on Good Friday, 1896, as she spat up blood. This trial opened a doorway to Thérèse: a doorway which would be the most difficult one yet, one which would accompany her right to her own death, and one which would be a trial of her faith.

In the Autumn of 1896, Thérèse wrote and edited Manuscript B, addressed to Jesus and to Sister Mary of the Sacred Heart. At the beginning of June 1897, at the request of Mother Mary Gonzaga, she worked to complete her memoirs in Manuscript C and revealed to all her inner thoughts in "last conversations."

Sister Thérèse of the Child Jesus and of the Holy Face reached her own personal Easter on the evening of September 30, 1897, surrounded by her Carmelite sisters in Lisieux. All her work had been achieved, but yet it had also just begun.

Thérèse's grave, in the Lisieux cemetery, would become a pilgrimage site. Thérèse's somewhat edited manuscripts were published in 1898 as *The Story of a Soul*. As a result, the Lisieux Carmelites were invaded with letters that came from all over the world. The canonical process for her beatification was begun in 1910. Thérèse of the Child Jesus was declared "blessed" on April 29, 1923 by Pope Pius XI and was canonized as a "saint" on May 17, 1925.

The thorns had disappeared, and now Thérèse spread her "rose petals" on earth like blessings granted by our Lord through his intermediary.

At the beginning of 1937, the basilica in Lisieux was blessed; it was consecrated in July 1954. Thérèse protected her Carmel throughout the bombings in World War II in the same way as she will always watch over the missionaries of the world. She who lived a cloistered life also lived a totally missionary life.

The publication of the original manuscripts that inspired *The Story of a Soul* shows the true face of Saint Thérèse of the Child Jesus and of the Holy Face. She is a saint for all times, whose message is an echo of the Gospel of our Lord as it is lived from day to day—through the barrenness of faith, through the trials of suffering, through the gift of love. In the often monotonous existence of ordinary everyday life, Thérèse, through the grace of God, has demonstrated the extraordinary nature of a love that can transform everything. She sums up her graced philosophy in this way:

> To live in love is to live Your life, glorious King....
> [It] is to look upon the Cross as a treasure....[It]
> is to banish all memory of past mistakes....[It] is
> to sail tirelessly, sowing peace and happiness into
> all hearts....To love you, Jesus, what a bountiful
> loss...I want to leave this world singing "I am
> dying of love."
>
> *Thérèse of Lisieux, PN 17*

References
and Abbreviations

THE THÉRÈSIAN TEXTS are taken from *The Complete Works of Thérèse of Lisieux*, published by CERF-DDB, 1992. Here is a guide to the abbreviations used:

LT 168 = Letter 168

Ms A, 45v = Manuscript A, folio 45, verso (or overleaf)

Ms B, 5r = Manuscript B, folio 5, recto (or front side)

Ms C, 16v = Manuscript C, folio 16, verso

O.C. = Complete Works

PN 17 = Poem number 17

DE 3.7.2 = *Last Conversations*, dated July 3, second recorded comment

CSG = *Advice and Memories*, Sister Geneviève

RP 3 = Carmel Theater, "Spiritual Interlude" No. 3

Pri 6 = Prayer number 6

Scriptural citations are taken from the *New Revised Standard Version Bible*.

Introduction

The Little One's Journey
Along the Way of Love and Holiness

WHY COULDN'T THÉRÈSE'S little way be our own?

To walk while holding onto the hand of the One who guides us so that, little by little, we gain some assurance and so that we are drawn onto the route of holiness which is the road of love.

Isn't it true that "God chose us in Christ before the foundation of the world to be holy and blameless before Him in love" (Eph 1:4). He "has now reconciled in his fleshly body through death, so as to present you holy and blameless and irreproachable before him" (Col 1:22). The God who is himself all holiness wants us to become saints, in his image, in order to present us in his kingdom of holiness, at the end of the road.

Thérèse of Lisieux felt the desire resound within herself as the music of holiness. She let it develop in her heart until it made her whole life into an offering of love. Just like a small child, she loved with complete confidence. Like a small child, she let herself be loved.

Thérèse's way of holiness included trials of suffering, self-abandonment, and daily offerings, all of which was included in the ultimate offering of Jesus, the mystery of the Eucharist.

The "way of love" was also discovered by Thérèse in her reading of the words of Saint Paul in 1 Corinthians, Chapter 13. It was this way of love which would unify her life. Thérèse at last understood that love encompasses all; she said: "I finally found my vocation, my vocation is love....[I]n the heart of the Church, my Mother, I will be love....[I]n this way, I will be everything" (Ms B, 3v).

Our own holiness will not be a copy of Thérèse's, but one which God wants to realize through us in the freedom of our love. That doesn't stop us from using Thérèse's way as a guide, a beacon, or a ray of hope.

To believe in love like a little child, to be in love, to live in love, brings us to the end of the road so that we can be consumed by Love, which is our earthly road toward the new world. As the writer of Revelation says: "Those who conquer will inherit these things, and I will be their God and they will be my children" (21:7).

The fifteen days of our journey with Thérèse are set out as follows:

Day One—Fascinated by Jesus
Day Two—A Little Flower of Love Despite Difficult Times
Day Three—Pushing Forward on the Road to Perfection
Day Four—Journey to Self-Abandonment
Day Five—The Living Desire for Sainthood
Day Six—My Path: To Love as You Love, O Lord
Day Seven—Love Beyond Sympathy
Day Eight—Days Without Sunlight and Happiness

From time to time, we may see bits of it through renewed sparks of love and offering, by welcoming the many loving favors given to us by God. But the only favor, in Thérèse's estimation, is to have "interludes of Divine Love" in our lives (Ms C, 8v), when all the earth would be assumed by love and consumed in love. Then the eternal day of God will open itself to us, a day of never-ending light where we can repeat our love to God, eternally and face to face. And in thanksgiving for the earthly route accomplished, we could only say with Thérèse: "I do not regret having given myself to love" (DE 30.9).

REFLECTION QUESTIONS

The Little Way seems to be a way that is much more difficult than what might first be imagined. Every choice, every desire, every impulse must be chosen and acted upon only because it gives glory and honor to God. It is an all-consuming way, a way that bends, molds, and finally shapes a person into a beautiful vessel that is pleasing to the Lord. What needs to be bended, molded, and finally shaped in you in order to pray, "I do not regret having given myself to love"?

15 Days of Prayer
With Saint Thérèse of Lisieux

DAY ONE
Fascinated by Jesus

FOCUS POINT

To be fascinated by something or someone is to experience being spellbound. It is the experience of having our intellect and our imagination focused, at the same moment, on the source of our fascination. Fascination is not a normal or everyday occurrence, and so, when it happens, it demands that we pay attention and that we respond.

My Jesus, I love you. I love the Church, my Mother. I remember that "the smallest act of pure love is more useful to her than all other deeds put together." But is pure love really in my heart?...Are my tremendous desires a dream, a fantasy?... Jesus, if they are, make this clear to me; you know I am seeking the truth....If my desires are foolhardy, make them disappear because, for me, these desires are the greatest of martyrs....In the meantime, oh Jesus, I feel that, after having hoped to attain the highest levels of love, if I am unable to reach them one day, I will have tasted more gentleness in my martyrdom, in my foolhardiness, than I shall experience in the happiness of my heaven, unless, through a miracle, you remove the memories of my earthly hopes. Then let me enjoy the delights of love through my exile. Let me savor the sweet bitterness of my martyrdom....

Jesus, Jesus, if it is so delightful to want to love you, what it must be like to possess and enjoy divine love!...How can an imperfect soul such as mine hope to have the fulfillment of divine love?

...Oh Jesus, my first and only friend, my only love, explain this mystery to me. Why don't you keep these immense desires for the great souls, for the eagles who soar to great heights?...Me, I consider myself only a weak little bird covered only with a light down. I am not an eagle; I only have the eyes and the heart of an eagle. In spite of my extreme smallness, I dare gaze at the Divine Sun, the Sun of Love. My heart feels, within itself, all the desires of the eagle....The little bird would like to fly toward that brilliant Sun which enchants its eyes. It would like to imitate its brothers, the eagles, whom it sees soaring all the way to the divine home of the Blessed Trinity....Alas, all it can do is lift up its wings, but to soar, that is not within its power.

What will it become? Will it die of despair from seeing itself so powerless?... Oh no, the little bird does not despair.... With bold abandon, it wants to remain fixed on its Divine Sun. Nothing will scare it off, not the wind, not the rain and if dark clouds should come to hide the Star of Love, the little bird will not move because it knows the Sun still shines behind those clouds and that its true brightness will not be overshadowed for one single moment.

Thérèse of Lisieux, Ms B, 4v–5r

The brilliant lights which would like to captivate our attention are numerous along our human paths. Their brilliance may be bright enough to even stop us along the pathway of life. Thérèse mourns:

The King of that shining homeland came to live in this land of darkness for thirty-three years. Alas! The darkness did not understand that this Divine King was the light of the world.

Thérèse of Lisieux, Ms C, 5v–6r

But we must believe this, even in our darkest hours, that beyond the clouds, the Divine Sun always shines, and we must "implore your favor [Jesus] with all our heart" (see Psalm 118 [119]:58). Only God's illuminated glance can draw our own. Only his magnificent beauty can enrapture us, captivate us, fascinate us. It is time for us to capture the rays of light which, by their beams, reveal the true source of light—Jesus arisen from the dead. But how can we get to this shining source which is so alive? How can we reach out to it?

The little bird, that frail little ball of feathers, can't soar to those heights. In our smallness, and by our own strength, how can we attain the realities that reside up above? That is the gist of it; it is in the weakness of the small that the strength of the heavens manifests itself. It is in the humble confidence of the smallest that the power of the love of our Lord can do its work.

The little bird "keeps its eyes fixed upon you. It wants to be mesmerized by your divine glance, it wants to fall prey to your love" (Ms B, 5v). It wants, not in a strong-armed way, but by the strength of the love it has in its heart. Love brings love, recognized love, the kind of love that is welcomed at the bottom of one's self. It is a love which becomes a gift of oneself just as a loving answer becomes so. It is a love which is given voluntarily, because the "Lord makes his face to shine upon us" (Ps 67:1). It is a love that is always growing if we have asked Jesus to "draw us into the flames of his love" (Ms C, 35v).

The little bird wants to be fascinated, captivated, and blinded by the sun of love, Jesus. But are these not foolhardy, reckless, impossible desires? Lord, you put this thirst to love you into the hearts of your children. Each of us does not live that pure love, but we can see the creation of the desire for it. The very desire to love you brings happiness, while spurned love brings sorrow. You made us for your happiness, for the happiness to love; if sorrow appears, it is a warning for us to return to the road toward heaven, our eyes riveted on the glorious light.

But how do we return to this route toward the heavens once again? We do so by having the desires of the eagles within ourselves, by having the eyes and the heart of an eagle, by having piercing eyes that fasten on the light and attract it to them, by having a strong heart that allows the eagle to rise above the mountain summits and straight to the brilliant source, by having a majestic flight that makes it easier to withstand the journey without tiring.

Only inner reflection, heightened by faith, will make us discover the divine home of the Blessed Trinity, since the Lord, after all, makes his home in us. Only a heart that beats in God's charity will find the strength to believe in love until it discovers it. Only those who rely upon the Lord can follow the road and persevere.

We must constantly "look to the Lord…and wait for the God of my salvation" (Mic 7:7), so that all of our weaknesses, which bind us to earthly things, can be removed.

The little sparrow doesn't understand the great flights of the eagle, but it is happy with its own small flights. The little sparrows of holiness do not look like the heroes of holiness, but each one lives in the light of love, according to its own degree of love. The weak little bird can, itself, also know the immensity of love. It marvels at what the Lord has created in the heart of the one who called herself "the little Thérèse," while having the eyes, heart, and the flight of "pure love." It is a road offered to us in our smallness and weakness which leads to the great heights of the heavens if we let ourselves be seduced (Jer 20:7) by the divine Sun and perceive the irresistible attraction within ourselves of his love.

It is not surprising if the little bird doesn't move. For it to be fascinated, does it not have to remain still in such a way so it can be captivated by the flash and the glance? We are ever-changing beings. How can we be fascinated and captivated? Without question, it is a given that consistency and perseverance are part of the road of life. An indispensable means of access to and establishment of love is to allow ourselves to be seduced and seized by Jesus, the one true light: "the dawn from on high," guiding our feet "into the way of peace" (Lk 1:78–79), the beacon of the new world (see also Rev 21:23). He who lives in the Church and walks along the route of Jesus will find himself coming across, at one time or another, its sun, Jesus, the divine Sun, and will then receive a new surge of love. And this movement of love will flash back upon the Church, which will permit it to be a reflection of the sun of love, a fascinating source of light and love which lifts us up and leads us to the heights of heaven.

REFLECTION QUESTIONS

In her perception of herself Thérèse perceived herself as the little bird, struggling toward the sun and not as the soaring eagle which seemed to reach the sun with little effort. How do you find yourself responding to her perception? Do you find it easy, or even appealing and helpful, to imagine yourself as little, or do you find yourself struggling with the idea? What is it in yourself that needs to be let go in order to become little? What fascinates you about your relationship with the Lord? What are the qualities in Jesus that you find most appealing?

DAY TWO

A Little Flower of Love Despite Difficult Times

FOCUS POINT

It is key to use your imagination in the spiritual journey. It is key to struggle with the images suggested by Thérèse and to discover a way to incorporate each image into your own spiritual experience in order to reap the full benefit offered by the saint. In this meditation, it is essential that you imagine yourself as a flower.

The older we get, the more we love Jesus. Because it is through Him that we love each other, then that is why our affection becomes so strong. It is more a unity than a union that exists between our two souls!...Céline, what must I say to you, don't you know everything? ...Yes, but I want to tell you why the Célines have blossomed earlier this year. Jesus made me feel it this morning for your birthday. Without a doubt, you have noticed that there has never been such a harsh winter as the one we had last year. As a result, the flowers have been late in blooming which is natural, and no one is surprised by that. But there is a mysterious little flower that Jesus has kept for himself in order to instruct our souls. This flower is Céline....

Contrary to all the others, she blossomed a month ahead of when she was expected to flower....Céline, do you understand the language of my precious little flower...the flower of my childhood...the flower of memories?...The harshness of the winter and the frosts have forced it to grow and flower instead of delaying it....This flower is so small and dull that no one paid any attention to it....Only the bees know about the treasures to be found in its mysterious blossom which is made up of a multitude of small petals, each of which is as rich as the other....Like the bees, Thérèse understood this mystery.

Winter is a period of suffering, an incomprehensible suffering, misunderstood, thought to be useless in the eyes of the impious, but it is rich and strong in the eyes of Jesus and the angels. Like the ever vigilant bees, they know to gather the honey contained in the mysterious and multiple petals which represent souls, or rather the children of the virginal little flower....Céline, I would need volumes to be able to write down all that I think about my little flower....To me, the flower is such a good image of your soul. Yes, Jesus did subject it to frosts instead of the warm sunshine of his consolations, but the effect he wanted did happen; the little plant grew and flowered almost all at once....Céline, when a flower blooms, all that is left to do is to pick it, but when and how will Jesus pick his little flower? ...Maybe its rose color shows that it will be the martyr?...Yes, I can feel the rebirth of my desires....Maybe Jesus wants that, after having asked, so to *speak, love for love, he again requests blood for blood, life for life.*

In the meantime, one must let the bees drain all of the honey from the flowers, leaving nothing and giving it all to Jesus. Then we will finally say, like the flower of the twilight of our life: "This is the evening." Then it will be over….And the gentle rays of the Sun will replace the frost, Jesus' eternal smiles will replace his tears.

Thérèse of Lisieux, LT 132, to Céline

W ho has never complained about the harsh weather when the snows and sleets of winter, all of a sudden, paralyzed life? Who has never complained about heat or tornados or floods, as if other times before our own had not known difficult trials? Who looks for a trace or a glimmer of life in the darkest hours? The more we surround ourselves with the darkness, the less we are available to receive the warmth and illumination of the light.

It is time to be the one who "walks in darkness and has no light, yet trusts in the name of the LORD and relies upon his God" (Isa 50:10). When we rely on the Lord and lean upon his Cross, which is a sign of hope, we will find the confidence we need to withstand the harshness of life, the cold and long winter nights. The little flower needs such support because it is so frail. Thérèse says: "If the dear Lord hadn't lavished his beneficial rays on his little flower, it would never have been able to adapt to earth…his blessings.…Jesus made it find them, even under the snow of hardship" (Ms A, 13v).

Oh, how disconcerting it is to encounter hardship along the way! It can strike suddenly, last a while and, just as suddenly, seem to stop. We would really like it to leave quickly. The hardship slows the blossoming of the flower, but it doesn't destroy it. We need time to grasp the meaning of the hardship so that we can withstand it, or we will understand nothing. In the same way as the snow protects the plants it covers, the hardship, when endured with confidence, will not eliminate life, will not destroy the small, frail plant that we are. We must "hold fast to love and justice," and wait continually for our God (Hos 12:6), in order to withstand the harshness of the trial.

Love has been given to us to the ultimate limit by Jesus on the Cross. "The little flower [could only] bloom in the shadow of the Cross" (Ms A, 71r), the tree of life. The sleep of death was a prelude to the resurrection into life. The sleep of winter, the harshness of the weather, will bring forth the blossoming of life. But experiencing the seasons doesn't necessarily bring about a human or spiritual experience.

And, aren't we truly alone during this hardship? No one pays attention to the very small and dull flower that we are. Really, no one? Yes, you do, Lord, when you told us: "Do not be afraid,…for I am with you" (Acts 18:9–10). But you are hidden under the snow of hardship. By trusting "in your steadfast love" (Ps 13:5), I will become able to open myself to the transforming love of the Lord, which will eventually overcome and melt the snow of hardship, even though sometimes the snow is so deep that it will take a long time to melt away.

Thérèse reminds us that only love will make us acceptable to God, and that love is the only thing to which we should aspire. Only love will allow us to withstand suffering, which is useless and vain for those who have no faith or understanding of the life in God. Isn't suffering somewhat like death, with its lack of meaning? The bees go to the petals of the flower to make their harvest so they can manufacture their invigorating honey. The Lord goes into the bruised flower of our heart, of our life, to gather all that he finds that is beautiful and good, while we, ourselves, see nothing of value.

We are just little flowers, not majestic trees in the forest; small, frail flowers, open to the hazards of the weather, but also offered to the divine Sun of love.

We are little flowers that exist to make the Lord happy. Thérèse points out: "The little flower bloomed in the shadow of the Cross; the tears and blood of Jesus became its dew and its Sun was his Adorable Face, veiled with tears" (Ms A, 71r).

Little flowers that we are, we discover God's strength and the depth of his love through the suffering of the Cross. Tears are shed in pain, but rich tears. It is a veiled sun, but it is always a warm, loving sun with transforming brilliance.

The little flower exists in the midst of other flowers who have also experienced frosts and the hardship of snow. When one wakes up and blooms, it is like a call that's sent to the others to open themselves to the dew of the Cross and the warm sun of Jesus.

Like Thérèse and Céline, we also can live a unity through the communion of hardship. But we must agree to become simple, little flowers, ones which could be hurt and crushed by a clumsy step but straightened and cared for by a brotherly, loving hand.

Proclaims Paul: "Power is made perfect in weakness...so I will boast all the more gladly of my weaknesses, so that the power of Christ may dwell in me" (2 Cor 12:9). We are weak on our own, and can be strengthened through Christ, as indeed we are. Furthermore, Thérèse points out in Letter 197 that "the more one is weak, without desires of virtues, the more one is ready for the workings of this burning, transforming love." It is in the same way that one grows and flowers. There, we will understand that all that is in us is of God's creation. But if we are not open to the strength of the love of Jesus, the little flower will die.

The little flower, at its very conception, is made to be picked by the divine gardener, for Thérèse avers: "Jesus will come get us, no matter how far away we are and change us into flames of love" (LT 197).

God will harvest all of his little flowers in the twilight of life, in the final hours. In the last hours of our life, a setting sun will open us up to an eternal day without sunset, enlightened by Jesus, the Sun of love, where "death will be no more; mourning and crying and pain will be no more, for the first things have passed away" (Rev 21:4). The little flower, in the midst of its brothers and sisters, will brighten up God's heaven in a heart-to-heart relationship with its Lord.

In the meantime, life goes on. One must drink of the dew of the Cross, keeping nothing for oneself, but give it all to Jesus. Then, in the flower of our heart, Jesus will drink of the honey of our love, of his "little flower of love."

REFLECTION QUESTIONS

How does it feel to be small and helpless, easily trampled underfoot or uprooted by any passerby? What have been the experiences in your life in which you have felt the most fragile, the most dependent? Can you discover the wisdom and the necessity of total dependence on God, the feeling of powerlessness, that is essential for the journey? Can you identify those parts of yourself that may need to become more vulnerable? What is the spiritual value of giving everything away and keeping nothing for yourself?

DAY THREE

Pushing Forward on the Road to Perfection

FOCUS POINT

There are many challenges that confront a person on the spiritual journey. The challenge that seems to be present more than any other is discouragement, especially the discouragement that comes from the feeling that a person is not progressing fast enough or skillfully enough. In this reflection, Thérèse counsels the need to move forward, regardless of how a person might feel.

Give grateful thanks to God for all of the graces he has given you and don't be so ungrateful that you do not recognize them! You act as if you are a little villager who, when the king proposes marriage, doesn't dare accept because she feels she is neither rich enough nor experienced enough in courtly manners, not taking into consideration that her royal fiancé knows about her poverty and weakness even better than she does herself.

Marie, if you are nothing, you must not forget that Jesus is everything. You must also lose your little nothing in his infinite everything and, from now on, think only of his uniquely lovable everything....We must stop wanting to see the fruits of our efforts; Jesus is happy to keep these little nothings for himself, they console him....You are mistaken, my dear, if you believe that your little Thérèse always walks earnestly along the path of virtue. She is so weak. Each day, she has a new experience along it but, Marie, Jesus is happy to teach her just as he taught Paul to boast of his infirmities. This is a great blessing. I pray that Jesus will teach you this because this is the only way you will find peace and rest for your heart. When we see ourselves so wretched, we no longer want to think of ourselves and want only to look to the unique Beloved!

My dear little Marie, I know no other way to achieve perfection than "love."...How well our heart is made for love!... Sometimes I try to find another word to express love, but in this land of exiles, words are powerless to express the feelings of the soul. One must hold on to this single, unique word: "love"!

But to whom will our poor deprived heart give its love?... Oh, who will be big enough for that?...Can a human being even understand it...and above all, would it be able to provide it? Marie, there is only one Lord who could understand the depth of the word "love"!...Only Jesus knows how to give us infinitely more than we give him.

Thérèse of the Child Jesus, LT 109

"Perfection is not for this world." This adage is not meant to lock us into mediocrity. Even though we live *in* this world, we are not *of* this world. We have been made for God's world, but how do we reach it? We must walk on and push forward, day after day, on the road to perfection, which is love.

We are on the road. Let us begin by recognizing all the fragments of love which have been scattered about over our route. Here is Thérèse's advice:

Your love advised me from as early on as my childhood; it grew with me, and now it is an abyss so deep that I can't measure its depth. Love attracts love....My love throws itself toward you.

Thérèse of Lisieux, Ms C, 34v–35v

B eing able to delve into and reflect on these marvelous gifts gives us the energy to move on and also provides us with an opportunity to give thanks. His love was the first gift. By discovering it, we are led to respond to his love. Whether it is a progressive or an overwhelmingly singular discovery, it is a discovery that always has a future: to grow in love received and in love already given. Ingratitude is not a fitting quality for someone who is moving along the road to perfection. It is a detour on our journey.

There is, however, in us sufficient weakness to slow us down or even stop us. We are not models of perfection. As Thérèse says: "I am only a child, powerless and weak. However, it is this weakness that gives me the boldness to offer myself as a sacrificial victim to your love, Jesus" (Ms B, 3v).

You know each of us better than we know ourselves, Lord;

you know our weaknesses, our many weaknesses. However, you still invite us to push forward. Our forward movement is your work in us. Thérèse lucidly points out: "I am not concerned when I see that I am weak. On the contrary, it is that weakness which glorifies me. Every day I expect to discover new imperfections within myself" (Ms C, 15r).

These following words will help our reflections: I am nothing on my own. Jesus, you are everything, so I want to lose myself in you. In your infinite all, I will become able to push forward in love. This is what you have asked of me: "You shall love the Lord your God with all your heart, with all your soul, and with all your might" (Deut 6:5). You ask for all, even when I am nothing, even when I am a sinner. Sin along my route could stop me, discourage me, and force me to say to myself: "You will never amount to anything." At this point, Thérèse throws all of us who would profit from her Little Way a lifeline:

> When I make a mistake which saddens me, I know that this sadness is the result of my unfaithfulness. Do you think I stop there? Oh no, I am not that silly. I hurry to say to God: Lord, I know that I deserve this feeling of sadness, but let me offer it to you anyway as a test you have sent me out of love. I regret my sin, but I am happy to have this suffering to offer up to you.
>
> *Thérèse of Lisieux, DE 3.7.2*

When we are in the depths of regret and a state of weakness, it is better for us to dive into the Beloved's fountain of love which flows from the Cross, so we can be revitalized through love. Thérèse advises: "Love can find a way to consume all that could displease Jesus, leaving a single but humble profound peace in our hearts" (Ms A, 83r). Regret will be fruitless if it doesn't lead to love.

Parents encourage their children to start something they will be able to finish. It is an incentive for them. On the road to perfection, we should not wait to see the fruit of our labors. Besides, what could we have done without God's help? We carry out all these taxing efforts to push forward toward you, as well as all these little nothings which seem to be important to us, for your sake, Oh Lord. If you give us a perception of the fruits of these efforts, we thank you. That will be an incentive. But if you want to keep these fruits hidden and reserved to yourself, we offer them to you. Are you not the "Divine Beggar of Love"? Would anyone truly love you if they didn't accept your gifts of love? You who are love, you who are only love, draw us after you, "let us make haste" (Song 1:4). Lead those of us who on love's road to perfection.

Just as the great saints knew their limits and weaknesses, we also must know our own. Is it possible to discover and see them even better when we have contact with you and can be close to you, Jesus. You have bestowed the grace to hear your call and your command: "Above all, clothe yourselves with love" (Col 3:14). Even if we must watch where we put our feet, you still ask us to join you, our only Beloved. Your loving glance is the assurance you give that we are on the right path, the road to perfection. Let us return your glance with love.

You require us to walk in all your ways, to love you, and to serve you (see Deut 10:12). You are, in that sense, the "Divine Beggar of Love," the one "who asks for hospitality and says 'thank you' by always asking for more in proportion to what he receives" (LT 172).

What we need is the knowledge of love, for it is then that love becomes the dynamic force of the road just as much as the goal. Thérèse says: "I understand completely that only love can make us acceptable to God. I strive only for that love" (LT 196).

Love is a sentiment that comes from the depths of the human heart; it is an emotion that is expressed in communion with other people, or within the marital bond, or in an honest and true friendship. Because of you, Lord, we are made for love. How else could we be made since we have been created in the image of the one Lord who is love, who is all love?

Love grasps us completely through the gift of ourselves and in the humble, confident welcome by the other. Love is a unique word which can never quite express the totality of our inner feelings. Love is a word that will not allow the other to become an object. Because love is a gift and a welcome to the gift, it does not seize someone against their will. Love is all.

No matter what our vocation is in the Church, Jesus' call reaches out to us: "If you come to me, without being ready to give up your love for your father and mother, your spouse and children, your brothers and sisters, and indeed yourself, you cannot be my disciple" (Lk 14:26).

The road to perfection demands that the first choice be love for Jesus, through whom all human love will find its road. To live in love, one must be brought to the very source of love: Jesus. Only he loved to the limits of love so that life is given to us through him. Only he gives of himself out of his endless bounty of love to steer us to the end and limits of perfection: the face-to-face of love in God's eternity.

REFLECTION QUESTIONS

Identify for yourself those moments and those qualities that make you feel good about your spiritual journey. List those qualities and moments that lead to frustration or anxiety. When you feel good how would you describe your prayer? When you are feeling discouraged are there distinct movements and happenings in your prayer that you can identify? Can you bring both the good moments and the not-so-good moments to the Lord in prayer today?

DAY FOUR

Journey to
Self-Abandonment

FOCUS POINT

To abandon self, to step back and to freely let go of the need to control everything about your life, to simply permit the experiences of life to come and go without attaching a particular interpretation or judgment to them, is extremely difficult. However, it is in the letting go that we best experience the necessary freedom for the spiritual journey.

Don't believe that I swim in consolation. Oh no, my solace is to have none on earth! Jesus, without showing me, or even making me hear his voice, teaches me in secret, not by using books, because I do not understand what I read. But, at times, guidance comes to me at the end of a prayer, like this one: "Here, I give you the teacher. He will teach you all you must do. I want to make you read from the book of life which contains all the knowledge about love." The knowledge of love, oh yes, these words echo gently in my soul. Having given up all my wealth, like the wife in the sacred canticles, I feel that I have given nothing....I understand completely that only love can make us acceptable to God. I strive only for that love. Jesus is happy to show me the only path to the divine blazing fire. This path is the self-abandonment of the little child who sleeps without fear in his father's arms....

"If someone is very small, let them come to me," said the Holy Spirit through Solomon's mouth. The same Spirit of Love again said "mercy is given to the little ones." In his name, the prophet Isaiah reveals to us that on the final day "the Lord will lead his troops into the pastures, he will assemble his little lambs and bring them to his breast." As if these promises weren't enough, the same prophet whose inspired thoughts plunged into the eternal depths, wrote, in the name of the Lord: "Like a mother caresses her child, I will console you in the same way, I will carry you next to my breast and I will hold you in my lap." O dear Godmother, hearing such words, there is nothing left to say only to cry in recognition and love....Oh, if all of the weak and imperfect souls could sense what I feel—that the soul of your little Thérèse is the smallest of them all, then not a single one of them would worry about arriving at the summit of the mountain of love. Jesus doesn't ask for great deeds, only self-abandon and recognition.

Offer God the sacrifices of praise and thanksgiving. That is what Jesus asks of us. He doesn't need anything else from us, only our love. This same God who declares having no need to tell us he is hungry is not afraid to beg for a little water from the woman at the well in Samaria. He was thirsty...but by saying "give me something to drink," the

Creator of the Universe was claiming love from his poor crea-
ture. He was thirsty for love....Oh, I feel it; Jesus is thirstier
than ever! He only encounters thankless and indifferent people
among his followers and disciples. Alas, among his disciples,
he finds few hearts given to him without reservation and who
understand the tenderness of his infinite love.

Thérèse of Lisieux, LT 196,
to Sister Mary of the Sacred Heart

S elf-abandonment like a little child: what difficulty does
this cause us, we who declare ourselves to be responsible
adults? It's as if we have to renounce who we are and what
we have become. We must understand that the Lord doesn't
send us on a road that will not build us up. It is up to us to
decode the language and the mystery it brings. It is up to us
to acquire the knowledge of love so that we can truly begin to
understand. It is up to us, above all, to let ourselves be taught.

The little one's self-abandonment is not learned by reading books, but in secret in the heart. The teacher is Jesus himself. Life experience is enlightening. It was the little ones, the
babies, the infants in their mothers' arms who were presented
to Jesus while he was on his route one day (see Lk 18:15).
What else could they do but cry? That was why the disciples
tried to keep them away. They felt secure, confident in their
abandonment to their mothers' arms. Jesus blessed them.
The road we should take is the same as these children; self-
abandonment, removal of self, all with complicit and loving
glances.

The knowledge of love for each of us is written in the
book of life. We must decode the signs. In tough times, Jesus

will give consolation to cradle the little ones so that they will follow the road. But in order to forge character and build personality, we must cry and not be consoled, for our solace is not to be had here on earth.

How can little ones live in self-abandonment? They can do so through the love they feel from their mothers and fathers. Loving gestures, gentle voices, and the glances that transmit love bring confidence and the courage of self-abandonment. A sense of security brings peace and calm. This is a road that indeed must be followed in love.

Come, then, to Jesus' school, all those who are "gentle and humble in heart" (Mt 11:29). Let us be steered on the Lord's road, having confidence in him that he will act. Hear him call out to have those who are small brought to him. "If someone is small, bring them to me." Let us come "to hide in his shelter" (Ps 27:5). When we are close to him, we will put our arrogance, our self-importance, and our self-assurance aside. It is by losing our sense of self that we will find freedom in Jesus.

There are so many things that attach us to ourselves. We have given nothing as long as we have not given ourselves up to the love of Jesus in the same manner as he gave us his supreme love by giving of himself on the Cross.

The one road which takes us to the living source of love is the one of the little child who, in an act of abandonment, sleeps without fear in the arms of his father. Thérèse's human experience with her father opened her heart to a spiritual attitude. It was the attitude of self-abandonment and confident surrender of her entire being which gave her profound peace. That is what we need for ourselves: "I have quieted and stilled my soul like a weaned child on its mother's lap; like a contented child is my soul" (Ps 131:2).

Thérèse tells us that in order "to belong to Jesus, one must make oneself small, as small as a dewdrop" (LT 141). This message is difficult to hear. The dewdrop will surely disappear at the slightest ray of sunshine, but by the warmth of the King of Light, it will bring enough humidity to the plants. One must be small, like a dewdrop, to be nourished by the divine sun of love.

Thérèse exclaims: "Oh, there are very few souls who aspire to stay that small!" (LT 141). It is the hour of truth for us. Do we choose the road of human grandeurs or the road of revealing humility? "The Lord brought down the powerful from their thrones and lifted up the lowly" (Lk 1:52). We are called to make our choices. We are called to choose the little one's road of self-abandonment.

"I am not always faithful," says Thérèse, "but I never get discouraged; I give myself up to Jesus' arms" (LT 143). Does he not walk with us, holding our childlike hands tightly in his love-empowered grip? And if we should fall, mercy is given to the little ones. Everything invites us to push onward, not with an adult sense of security, but in childlike and humble confidence.

The God of love never stops watching lovingly over each of his children. He waits for us to return his glance. In the difficult times, he encourages us with his hopeful word. In times of distress, he comforts us with his inner presence. In times of gladness, he lifts us up to greater heights of love. In the same way as the shepherd goes to find the lost sheep who has strayed from the flock and may be in danger, so, too, Jesus comes to us and opens his merciful and tender heart.

Didn't Jesus make himself become a little one in the manger in Bethlehem? Did he not give himself up in abandon to the arms of Mary and Joseph? Fear not! He knows all about self-abandonment. And what more could we say about his supreme act of self-abandonment than when he was on the Cross? "Into your hands I commend my spirit, O Lord" (Ps 31:5). It is from him that we can learn about self-abandonment, the total giving of oneself to the Lord, for as Thérèse points out: "He teaches me do to everything through love, to refuse him nothing...in peace, without consideration" (LT 142).

It goes without saying that we must act to prove our abilities to ourselves and to serve those around us. It is true. Each one of us must increase the skills we have been granted, but we must do this without bringing glory upon ourselves. Only love gives value to what we achieve, in the same way as a little one who "stays close to the throne of the king and queen of love in the place of his brothers who go out and fight" (Ms B, 4r).

In our relationships with others, through joy and sorrow, we learn the full dimension of love. We must love like the little ones, without motive, through the total relinquishment of ourselves.

The Lord waits for only one thing in order to give full value to our existence: he only wants our love, the gift of ourselves, the offering of all that we have in the divesting of our sense of self. Then, his love will gather all of these humble gifts along our road so he can transform them into pearls of love, but only if we understand his tenderness and give to him without reservation, certain that he "would not leave us alone in a time of danger" (LT 258). On our road to self-abandonment, we must remember the plea of Psalm 17:8: "Keep me under the shadow of your wings and hide me."

REFLECTION QUESTIONS

How do I define myself? Is there something about myself, a title, a position, a particular skill or talent, that I am convinced is necessary in order for me to be me? Can I imagine not possessing it? Can I imagine freely laying it down before the feet of the Lord? How do I feel as I lay it down and abandon it? What particular grace fills the spot that was once occupied by this perceived necessity?

DAY FIVE

The Living Desire for Sainthood

FOCUS POINT

Every person has a goal in life, something that they desire in order to feel complete and accomplished. More often than not the goal demands more learning, more discipline, more energy in order to be attained. Upon reflection most goals might seem to be ordinary, that is, when compared to the personal goal of becoming a saint!

Oh Lord, Blessed Trinity, I want to love you and make you loved, to work toward the glorification of the Holy Church by saving souls on earth and by delivering those who suffer in purgatory. I want to fulfill your will perfectly and come to the level of glory which you have prepared for me in your kingdom: in short, I would like to become a saint, but I feel my powerlessness. I ask you, my Lord, to be my saintliness.

Because you have loved me to the point of giving your only Son to me as my Savior and Spouse, the infinite treasure of his graces are also mine. I gladly offer these to you, begging that you look at me only through the Holy Face of Jesus and in his burning heart.

Once again, I offer you all the graces of the saints (those in heaven and on earth), their acts of love and those of the holy angels; finally, I offer you, O Blessed Trinity, the love and the merits of the Blessed Virgin. I send my offering to her, and ask her to present it to you. During the days of his earthly life, her Divine Son, my blessed spouse, told us, "All that you ask of my Father in my name, he will give you." Thus, I am certain that you will grant my desires. This I know, O Lord: the more you give, the greater the desire you create. In my heart, I feel great desire. With all confidence, I ask you to come take possession of my soul. I can't receive holy Communion as often as I would like, but Lord, aren't you all powerful?…Remain with me, as you do at the tabernacle. Do not ever leave your little host….I want to console you for the ingratitude of wicked people.

I beg you to take away from me the freedom to displease you. If I occasionally stumble out of weakness, I ask that you quickly purify my soul by your divine glance, removing all my imperfections, like a fire that consumes everything within its flames.

Thérèse of Lisieux, Pri 6

D oes this thought sometimes occur to you: being a saint is not for me? However, no one can be welcomed into God's world without first being on good terms with him through the fruit of his blessings. We are all called to saint-hood, a sainthood which is perfected, day after day, on the road of life.

"I desire," said Thérèse. The desire to live helps us live. The desire to be a saint brings us closer to sainthood, for as Isaiah says, "My soul yearns for you in the night, my spirit within me earnestly seeks you, Lord" (26:9), and "Your name and your renown are the soul's desire" (26:8).

Lord, it is you who plants this desire in my soul. It is you who makes sure that "all my longing is known to you" (Ps 38:9). To amputate my desires would be to remove all sparks of life, all profound hope. Lord, help me keep my desire for sainthood, my thirst for you, the living God, the God of all holiness. I know that you will give me what you make me desire, for "as a deer longs for flowing streams, so my soul longs for you, O God" (Ps 42:1).

Lord, keep me thirsty for sainthood. Give me the grace to contemplate you in the mystery of profound sainthood—Father, Son, and Holy Spirit—until I am able to contemplate you to the degree of glory that will be my own, that will reflect my degree of love for you along my road.

The desire for sainthood is a loving reply in the present. The desire for sainthood is my "yes" to your loving will for me. It is a desire which your saintly being finds dwelling inside me to transform me through you.

It is not enough to simply desire to be a saint? What must we do to become one? To begin with, we must let ourselves be loved by the one who is love, who is only love, Jesus: God's loving gift to humankind, the fruit of the loving Spirit of the Virgin Mary, the loving gift to the Father and to the entire human race. We must let ourselves be loved to learn how to love as God loves. Then we must let ourselves be seen by the Father through the Holy Face of Jesus, the bruised face of the agony, the beautiful shining face of the Transfiguration. Finally, we must let ourselves be cradled in the burning heart of love of the one who was crucified, so that we can be transformed by the Holy Spirit in flames of love.

If this great feat isn't for me, perhaps I am afraid to go that far. Who am I compared to the hero-saints, the martyrs for the faith? Saint Thérèse tells us: "I always realized when I compared myself to the saints, that the differences between us were as great as those between a mountain peak hidden by clouds and a single grain of sand underfoot to those passing by" (Ms C, 2v).

True, but all the grains added together make a pile and it is that pile which is important. The heart of God rejoices in the sainthood of the little ones. The degree of glory corresponds to the degree of love given by the saints. They are as varied in love and in glory as is God's creation in its diversity of colors and life.

Thérèse tells us: "God wanted to create great saints who could be compared to lilies and roses, but he also created lesser saints. They should be content to be daisies and violets, destined to simply enjoy God's glance as they lie humbly at his feet" (Ms A, 2v).

How wonderfully Thérèse points out that, in God's heaven, no one is jealous of one another. Each contemplates how God's keen desire is achieved in the light of glory. The abundant variety of colors reflect the welcome of the gift of love in each—and each person's own response to that love. Such a marvelous diversity of God's gifts! The greatness of human freedom opens to divine love. Our sainthood will make God happy.

The desire for sainthood pushes us ahead. The desires that

God puts into our souls are not impossible to realize, but our desires will not be quenched unless it is through him. Thérèse assures us that we can aspire to sainthood in spite of our smallness. Is not everything within us a work of God? "You guide me with your counsel, and afterward, you will receive me with honor" and "You hold my right hand" (Ps 73:24) in order to steer me to you.

By following the Lord, we learn that sainthood is always growing within us, right up until the time of our supreme passage toward the sainthood of God. Thérèse explains in Letter 83: "Jesus does not want to put a limit on sainthood....His own limit is that there is none"; and "The love that Jesus has for us is a love that asks for it all."

There is no "sale" price for sainthood; this is because we don't love in half measures. That would not be love. Thérèse proclaims that she does not want to be a halfway saint; she chooses it all: all that God wants, she wants. That would not be responding in the fullness of love.

The way to respond to the will of God is to make ourselves hear his loving calls. Our sainthood will not come about without our cooperation. The road to sainthood is rough. It is true, as Thérèse says: "Holiness doesn't consist of saying nice things, it does not consist of thinking them...it consists of suffering, and suffering for it all" (LT 89). Sainthood imposes a choice between legitimate things. Choosing the best may force us to make a choice in favor of something which has little interest to us, even in the small things. God is not sadistic to the point of making the road to sainthood a way of suffering. It is up to us to choose where we place ourselves, through the choices that must be made.

Thérèse understood that to become a saint, one must suffer a great deal; one must always seek perfection and forget one's self. To flee mediocrity, to reject half measures, to avoid making oneself the center of it all, is that not suffering on our road? Corporal suffering, the dark nights of faith, could also happen. Thérèse also understood that to live in smallness was a particular dimension of sainthood.

Even if our sainthood cannot be achieved without us, it is also not of our own doing. What will my weak efforts be, in the face of such a task? Thérèse so beautifully reassures us: "It is Jesus alone, content with my feeble efforts, who will lift me to his side and, covering me with his infinite virtue, he will make a saint of me" (Ms A, 32r).

In order that all our desires for sainthood come true, you take them, Lord, in your unique offering. Keep us as a humble gift of love for yourself. Consume us in the fire of your love. With Mary, the angels, and the saints of heaven, we aspire to sing your glory, O Beloved Trinity.

REFLECTION QUESTIONS

How has my personal understanding of sanctity changed as a result of this meditation? Can I recognize the individual call to holiness in the events and circumstances of my life? Is sainthood a realistic path for me? With God's help, would I be willing to pay the price?

DAY SIX

My Path: To Love as You Love, O Lord

FOCUS POINT

Human beings seem to love conditionally. Even with practice and conscious effort, there is a part of ourselves that often wonders, "What am I going to get out of all of this?" Perhaps this is why we find ourselves struggling to believe when we experience the unconditional love of Jesus.

How did Jesus love his disciples and why did he love them? It wasn't their human qualities that attracted him; an infinite distance existed between them. He was knowledge, eternal wisdom; they were poor sinners—ignorant, filled with worldly thoughts. Yet, Jesus calls them his friends, his brothers. He wants to open his Father's kingdom for them and see them reign with him in this kingdom. He wants to die on the Cross, having said: "There is no greater love than to give one's life for those we love."

Beloved Mother, upon meditating on the words of Jesus, I understood just how imperfect my love for my sisters was. I saw that I didn't love them the same way our Lord did. Oh, now I understand that perfect charity is composed of enduring others' faults, not being surprised by their weaknesses, and being happy to see them do even the smallest acts of virtue; but, above all, I understand that charity must not remain locked up in one's heart: Jesus said that no one lights a candlestick to put it under a bushel; so here we put it in a chandelier so that it lights up all those who are in the house. It seems to me that this candlestick represents charity which should shed light on and delight not only those people who are dearest to me, but all those in the house, without exception.

When God ordered his people to love their neighbor as themselves, he had not yet descended to earth. Also, knowing how much we love our own person, he could not ask his creatures to give an even greater love to their neighbor. But when Jesus gave his apostles a new commandment, his own commandment, as he later stated, he was not asking that they love their neighbor as themselves per se, but to love their neighbor as he, Jesus, has loved them, and as he will love them, until the end of time.

Lord, I know that you ask nothing that is impossible; you know better than I of my weakness, my imperfection, you know very well that I could never have loved my sisters as you love them if you, Jesus, didn't love them again in me. Because you would like to give me this grace, you have made a new commandment.

Thérèse of Lisieux, Ms C, 12r–12v

D oesn't the type of attitude shown in the preceding passage seem somewhat pretentious? It would if it were coming from one who has not traveled far on the road to sainthood. But it is God who calls us to love, to love in the same way as he loves, not in our own way. Thérèse says that the "meaning of love is to sacrifice yourself….God created children who know nothing and are only able to utter weak cries" (Ms A, 2r–3v). We are but children. Jesus provided a testimonial to the necessity for this humility on the evening of the Last Supper: "So if I, your Lord and Teacher, have washed your feet, you also ought to wash one another's feet" (Jn 13:14). Our act of becoming small has taken us to the ultimate limit of love, removing all barriers and opening ourselves to the Cross. This example teaches us that we must lower ourselves and place ourselves on the same level as others so as to avoid looking down on them. Before giving us the commandment of love—love your neighbor as yourself, as you have loved me—we experienced that same love in ourselves.

Jesus revealed the source of his love, the Father, from whom all perfect things come. His filial prayer was a prayer of love. And when the time came to choose his twelve disciples, he prayed. His choice was a loving, confident choice. All of God's choices are loving choices, inasmuch as he is the embodiment of love.

From the beginning, we may be ignorant and full of worldly thoughts. The Lord, who is all knowledge, knows this; he knows how to lead us, in freedom, to discover the route to him and to bind us to it. The Lord is wisdom; he knows how to give us a taste of his loving presence—a taste that will open us to love. The Lord works through our flaws to find our heart. At the beginning of our journey, Thérèse says: "He is happy with just a glance, a sigh of love" (LT 191). He is always the one to take the first steps, the one who loves us first so that he may bring us up to his heights of love. His project is to introduce us to the depths of love which rule in the very heart of the Trinitarian life of the Father, the Son, and the Holy Spirit. He marks out the road of love with his staff of love, the Cross. He opens the door to the kingdom through his resurrection from the dead. He wants us with him forever in his kingdom of love and peace.

Jesus has said: "No one has greater love than this, to lay down one's life for one's friends" (Jn 15:13). Lord,.so that I can love like you, give me access to your own love which will be the dynamic force on my road of love and progression to the Father. It is only you, Jesus, who could understand the depth of the word love. Open my thinking and heart to love.

We must love as God loves; we must love God as God loves us. Thérèse points out: "In order to love you as you love me, I must borrow your own love....Oh Jesus...I dare to ask you to love those whom you have given me in the same way as you have loved me" (Ms C, 35r). Our promise must be: Always "the how," in your same way, Lord.

Jesus didn't let the weaknesses of the twelve stop him: their presumptions, ambitions, pretensions, misunderstanding, even betrayal. In spite of this, he called each "my friend." We are prisoners of our own externalized thinking—a thinking that changes into interior judgment. We minimize our faults, our imperfections, while we exaggerate those of other people. This could not be a road of love. Must one then be neither clear-headed nor true to be able to love? Love is within the truthfulness of each of us. Betrayal is not love.

We must change our way of thinking from that of a person who weighs each choice, maneuvers, or makes snap judgments on sight, to that of a person who forgives and loves. What about the faults we see in others? True, they are there, but that is the flip side. And what if we learn only to see that side—the side of others' weaknesses? For, after all, they are there, right in front of us. But it is only by becoming supportive—by becoming a person on whom others can lean, that we will begin to love others.

Those little, simple acts of kindness and love are right there, but to really be able to see them, one must have a ready smile and a certain depth of love, for the Lord said, "I desire mercy, not sacrifice" (Mt 9:13). Our mercy and benevolence toward others will melt away even the hardest of shells, all our annoyances, and our quick, surface judgments because it affects us right to the deepest inner core of ourselves, in the same way as God affects us. Furthermore, only the person to whom we have shown mercy can understand it and live it, in his or her own way, for his or her brothers and sisters.

We can see the birth, in ourselves, of this will to equalize, so to speak, by the loving responses given to each person, using our own yardstick. Thérèse wrote: "I realized there were degrees of spiritual perfection and that every soul was free to respond to our Lord's invitation by doing a little or a great deal for him; in short, to choose from the sacrifices he asks of us" (Ms A, 10r–v).

If God truly respects the freedom of each of his children, how can we not imitate him? To be true, love must always occur out of a freedom to choose it. There is a marvelous variety in the various degrees of each person's love. Through this, the Lord can measure of the generosity of his children, from the humblest to the greatest. Since Thérèse says that love is a torrent that eliminates everything in its path, we must always draw from the true source to free ourselves from those things that may cool down our assent to love, that may stop us from seeing little bits of love in our neighbors' hearts and lives. For always, the indication of a disciple is this: "to love one another." Says Saint Paul in Romans, "Let this be the only debt of one to another: love" (13:8).

The charity which God gives us is like a shining beacon, always guiding us by the hand so that we can perceive the love of God along our road, to be able to live in and of it. It is the light which shines in our eyes and that reflects back on all those who cross our path along our way.

He gave us this new commandment in his offering, in the evening of his human life, on the Cross: "Love one another as I have loved you" (Jn 15:12). Love others, not only as you love yourselves, but as you have loved me and never stop loving. This means right to the ultimate limit of love, through the total consumption of our being by the Son of all human-kind.

How will we be able to follow Jesus? We must love others through Him. Are we faced with the impossible? No, because the new commandment, says Thérèse, "gives me the confidence that your will, oh Jesus, is to love, in me, all those you ask me to love" (Ms C, 12v). True love always calls us to bare our souls and give generously of ourselves.

REFLECTION QUESTIONS

What are the stumbling blocks within me that consistently make it difficult for me to love as Jesus loved? Am I willing to ask the Lord to engulf me, surround me, and free me from all such obstacles? Do I believe that the power of God's grace is powerful enough in me to permit me to love as Jesus loved?

DAY SEVEN
Love Beyond Sympathy

FOCUS POINT

It is easy to love those who love us. It is easy to love people who are attractive, talented, or humorous. It is not always easy to love people with whom we feel that we have little in common with or to whom we feel little attraction. It is very difficult to communicate with someone that we prefer not to be in relationship with.

Remembering that charity covers all sins, I draw from that plentiful source which Jesus has made available to me. In the Gospels, the Lord explains his new commandment. In the Gospel of Matthew, he says: "You have heard that it was said 'you shall love your neighbor and hate your enemy.' But I say to you, love your enemies and pray for those who persecute you." Surely, one does not encounter any enemies at Carmel. But there are affinities: you feel attracted to a certain sister, while you are willing to go to great lengths to avoid another.

Thus, without being aware of it, one becomes a subject of persecution. Well, Jesus tells me that I must love that sister and that I must pray for her, even if her behavior leads me to believe that she does not love me: "If you love those who love you, what credit is that to you. For even sinners love those who love them" (Lk 6:32).

And it is not sufficient just to love, you must prove that love. We are naturally happy to give a present to a friend, even happier to give surprise gifts, but that is not charity, even sinners do that. Jesus also teaches: "Give to everyone who begs from you; and if anyone takes away your goods, do not ask for them again" (Lk 6:30). To give to all those who ask is less sweet than offering oneself by an act of the heart. When we are asked kindly, giving seems to cost nothing. But, if by misfortune, one doesn't use kind words, immediately the soul would rebel if it isn't convinced of its charity. The uncharitable sister finds a thousand excuses to refuse what is asked of her; and it is only after noting the boldness of the person making the request, that she finally grants what is requested, or provides the small service that would have taken twenty times less effort to render than it took her to make a fuss about it. However, if it is difficult to give to whomever asks, it is even more so to let someone take a possession without reclaiming it. Oh, I say that it is difficult, but I should see that it just seems difficult, since the Lord's burden is a pleasant and easy one. When we accept it, we immediately feel its tenderness and cry out with the psalmist: "I have charged down the road of your commandments ever since you opened my heart." Only charity could open my heart. Oh Jesus, ever since this gentle flame began to consume [my heart], I happily follow the road of your new commandment.

Thérèse of Lisieux, Ms C, 15v–16r

D o we have as much sympathy for others as we might claim to have in certain circumstances? If, for us, sympathy is only a word that is not felt, it will be obvious, we will fool no one. In itself, sympathy is either a physical or moral attraction to another person with whom we feel a certain special connection. Sympathy can begin spontaneously within us, or it can grow gradually through time to a point where we share joy and sadness in friendship.

Sympathy is not the same as charity. One is based on sentiment, while the other is based on a gift from God that makes us love others in him. Without necessarily reaching the point of antipathy, we sometimes admit that we have no affinity for a given person. It means that sentiment still prevails in us. We are called to love beyond sympathy, beyond the attraction we might feel.

We will, undoubtedly, encounter people who will irritate us by their behavior and actions. Even Thérèse admits: "In the religious community, there is a sister who displeases me in all that she does, her mannerisms, her words, her character seems disagreeable to me" (Ms C, 13v). Antipathy will grow in us if we do not counter it. We must go beyond what is visible. "I told myself that charity should not consist of sentiments, but of deeds" (Ms C, 3v), reflects Thérèse. Thus, charity must be truly embedded in our attitudes toward the other person. As the Gospel says, "Little children, let us love, not in word or speech, but in truth and action" (1 Jn 3:18).

Sometimes, what we feel misleads us. It keeps us from reaching the truth that lies in the very depths of our being, stopping us at the surface. The exterior is not always a reflection of the interior. As Thérèse points out: "Jesus, artist of the souls, is happy when we don't stop at the outer layer, but delve deeper, right to the inner core of the soul, where Jesus has chosen to live, and where we can admire his beauty" (Ms C, 14r).

Truly, if we consider that each of us carries the presence of God inside, and if we meet the Trinitarian God who dwells in the hearts of believers, we go beyond sympathy and we live charity. This is what draws us: Jesus, who is hidden in the depth of the soul; Jesus, who can sweeten what is most bitter.

Love given through charity may sometimes be bitter or unattractive. It may not be the devil, but there is nothing present to establish a connection between the persons involved. It will, above all, become rejection, which then develops a bitter taste in us for charity. We must learn, as Luke says, "to lend, expecting nothing in return" (Lk 6:35). We must act to love in freedom.

To love those who love in return seems simple. We must look a little closer to see if we truly love others or, if instead, we love ourselves in that person, bringing everything back to ourselves, like an object to be admired.

The other person could also become an object of suffering for me, without my even knowing it. What can be done to counter that? As Saint Thérèse says, "When the devil tries to show my soul the flaws of another sister...I rush to find her virtues" (Ms C, 12v–13r). This can be done by changing the way I look at someone and adding a few drops of charity which will free me from possible antipathy. Praying for someone else is also a way to regain peace. We should not offer just any prayer, but the one which reinforces our feelings of charity and frees us from ourselves. Otherwise, it would simply be a facade and not real.

It is not enough just to love, we must prove it. Saint Thérèse alludes to this fact: "I was not satisfied just to pray for the sister who gave me so many battles. I tried to do all the favors I possibly could for her. When I was tempted to reply in a disagreeable way, I would just give her my most loving smile and try to change the subject" (Ms C, 14r).

To act on something is always liberating. It stops us from brooding about a difficulty and from letting it turn into resentment, thus confusing us. We sometimes lose time by asking ourselves what is wrong with someone or what we could have done differently. But we are called to live in "a unity of spirit, sympathy, love for one another, a tender heart, and a humble mind" and not "repay evil for evil and abuse for abuse" (1 Pet 3:8–9). Every single act should be done out of charity.

If someone else exasperates you occasionally, understand that you also do the same to them at times. We do not always draw sympathy to ourselves because of who we are, our attitudes, and our responses. Learn to take advantage of the lessons Thérèse has taught us: "We should be very happy that our neighbor denigrated us at times, because if no one did so, what would we become? It is to our advantage" (CSG 18). Even if our neighbor's comments are exaggerated, we will find some grain of truth in them. It is a way to grow as a person, to better our attitudes, to strengthen our character, to gauge our own love and humility.

Thérèse often said that a word or a friendly smile was often all it took to soothe a sad soul. She practiced this as a special expression of a type of sympathy. But even friendly smiles could engender a totally unexpected response: "Even the nicest words," admitted Thérèse, "may be misinterpreted" (Ms C, 28r). That turn of events is discouraging, and it may make us turn our back on someone. The best way to live, observes Thérèse, and not waste time, is "to be loving to everyone." A smile will brighten up our face and bring another person to return our smile with one of his or her own, as long as it is a genuine smile of peace and not simply a facade. No one should make the mistake of trying to paste a phony smile on a frowning face.

We say that there isn't love without some kind of gift, without an expression of the graces which are part of ourselves. Giving a surprise gift is not charity. Thérèse points out that it "isn't enough to give to those who ask, we must anticipate their needs. We must look honored and pleased to be of service" (Ms C, 17r). To be of service to others is a form of charity. The supreme service Jesus gave on the Cross was the greatest proof of his love. We must walk in the Master's footsteps.

We can make ourselves pray that we will be able to give, to understand that we are the giver and the other person is obligated to us, but this is neither sympathy nor charity.

The feeling must be a part of our being, something to be mastered, not to be despised. Without charity, who could draw upon the source, which is God. The new commandment draws its eternal youth from the source of love, Jesus, who loved us. The Lord loves us; he doesn't have sympathy for us. He calls us to love beyond and through his own love.

REFLECTION QUESTIONS

Who are the people that you find most difficult to love? Can you bring each of these people before the Lord in prayer? Can you identify the personality characteristics and traits that you do not find appealing in another? Can you also bring this to the Lord in your prayer?

Days Without Sunlight and Happiness

FOCUS POINT

When everything is going our way, when our cares and your concerns seem light, it is easy to believe and to continue the spiritual journey. However, there are times that we should expect that the journey will not be pleasant and even may be challenging. We have to learn to take the good moments and the difficult moments together.

What would you like to receive for your birthday? If I could get my wish, I would ask Jesus to send me all the woes, sorrows, and problems in the life of my beloved Céline. But you see, I don't give in to my whims, because I'm afraid that Jesus will tell me I'm selfish. I would like him to give me the best of what he has without leaving any for his little fiancée, whom he loves so much. He is proving his love for her by making her suffer from the separation, so I can't ask him for that. Also, he is so rich, so rich that he has enough to keep us both happy....

When we think of it, even if God gave us the whole universe, with all its treasures, it would not even compare to the smallest hardship. That is, I would happily refuse all the treasures of the world than give up even the smallest chance to suffer for him. What a blessing, when in the morning we feel no courage or strength to practice virtue, we realize it is then time to set the axe to the tree; instead of wasting time gathering a few sequins, we draw from our precious gems. What great benefits we will reap at the end of the day....True, at times, we resist building up our treasures for a few instants. That is a difficult moment. We are tempted to give up, but in an unnoticed act of love, all is restored: Jesus smiles. He is helping us without showing it. The tears he sheds for sinners are wiped away by our humble, weak love for him. Love can do it all; it finds that even the most impossible things are easy to achieve. Jesus does not measure the greatness or even the difficulty of our deeds, but the love that inspires us to do them.

I have recently come across a statement that should please you. Here it is, I believe you will find it beautiful: "Self-abandonment is still distinct from the will of God. It is the same as the difference between union and unity. In union, we are two persons, while in unity, we are only one." Yes, let us be one with Jesus, let us disregard everything else. Our thoughts must be turned only to heaven, since that is where Jesus lives.

Thérèse of Lisieux, LT 65, to Céline

Along our journey, there are days when we see everything as being black, days when we feel like doing nothing except being discouraged. We trod along as if we are in a long, dark, endless tunnel. We must recognize, as does Thérèse, that this is the lot of each and every one of us here on earth. "It is a great trial to see everything black, but this doesn't completely depend upon you; do what you can...then be assured that Jesus will do the rest" (LT 241). We see everything as being black because of life's troubles and worries; at times, heavy responsibilities rest on our shoulders. They are truly there; we can't pretend they're not. But this is the time when we should hear in our hearts that the Lord "gives power to the faint and strengthens the powerless" (Isa 40:29). It is up to us to find this strength and power even through the darkness. It is up to us to ask if we are truly on the right path.

Sometimes, without thinking, we take the dark path, the wrong path, which is not God's path for us. "I will lead the blind by a road they do not know, by paths they have not known, I will guide them. I will turn the darkness before them into light" (Isa 42:16). If the day is without sunshine, is it so because God isn't there or because I don't know how to find him through the darkness of my sorrow, pain, and suffering?

The Lord is there when we cry out: Where are you, Lord? Thérèse gives us this assurance: "Yes, life costs; it is difficult to start a day of hard work....If only we could feel Jesus...but no, he appears to be a thousand miles away. But what is that gentle friend doing? Doesn't he see the heavy burden that weighs us down? Where is he?. Why doesn't he come to comfort us as he is our only friend?" (LT 57).

What else can we do but cry out in distress? Yet again, instead of throwing ourselves once more into the shadows, we must search deep within ourselves, beyond the blackness.

We will end up discovering that God is there, very near, and he begs us for this sadness because he needs it for the souls in purgatory.

He waits for us to unload our sadness on him so that he can transform it into bits of grace and love for others who cry out for him. There is a ray of hope and a bit of joy left for us. If each person keeps his or her own sadness and worries bottled up inside, closing them off, this will lead to nothing. But if we open ourselves to the richness of Christ's love, he will, sooner or later, show us the light. He has something to enrich each and every one of us.

Thérèse declares that the "smallest bit of suffering is more valuable than all the treasures of the world." How, do we wonder, can it be a blessing to start a day without even enough courage or strength to serve the Lord? The blessing is not in the hardship itself, but in the lesson the Lord gives us to help us through it. It is a lesson given in the darkness of the blackest night, in the day without sunshine. Thérèse gives this one bit of advice: "There is only one thing to do during the darkest night, which comes but once in a lifetime. It is to love, to love Jesus with all the strength of our heart" (LT 96). Loving, in truth, will bring us out of ourselves by opening us up to others; and by welcoming them we welcome ourselves back from the dark abyss.

Sometimes the day without sunshine comes as a result of our refusal to separate ourselves from our invasive and darkened self. The light and happiness are outside of ourselves. Says Thérèse, "At times, we are so uncomfortable within ourselves, we must quickly reach out. Our Lord doesn't force us to stay within ourselves; oftentimes, he allows us this discomfort so we can reach out. I see no other way, in this case, than to reach outside of ourselves" (CSG 99).

We must reach outside of ourselves so that we don't become prisoners of ourselves and of the dark night along our life's path into which we have been plunged. We must reach out to see the light of day, the precious gems of our lives, because these gems can only shine in the light. They are precious gems of love and of the presence of Jesus inside us. They are precious gems of our love for him, seen through the acts of charity we have done. They are precious gems of the light of faith which reveal the virtues along the road. They are precious gems of rediscovered happiness, thanks to the presence of the Father, Son, and Holy Spirit within us.

Thérèse concludes, "Happiness is not found in the things around us. It is found in the secrecy of the soul. One could have it as well in a prison as in a palace" (Ms A, 65r). Happiness which is born out of the smallest act of love and confidence makes God happy. Nothing is too small when it is done out of love. The Lord doesn't expect difficult, heroic acts. He hopes that our love, no matter how small it is, can transform the darkness into bits of light until the beam they create is strong enough to shine through all darkness. How could we not beg with Esther: "O my Lord, help me, who am alone and have no helper" (Add Esth 14:3).

Are we destined to be resigned to this, bowing under the weight of hardships? Resignation has never been an evangelical virtue. Must we submit ourselves to the will of God? Yes, even if we don't succeed on the first try. From rejection, to welcoming God, to the offering of oneself is a long road to travel without light and happiness. But what God asks of us is to not give up when we are battle-fatigued, not to be discouraged. He will direct us to the light.

Sometimes, aren't we the cause of our own sorrows? Thérèse remarks: "There are those who perceive things in a way that gives them the most sorrow. For me, it is the opposite...if the sky is so dark that I see no light, good! I draw my happiness from it....I feast on it!" (DE 27.5.6).

We must incorporate the unity of our life into a communion with God so that we can live in unity with God. The end of our road is to be one with God, to live with him in his kingdom, in the glory of heaven.

But a veil of faith can fall on us, as well as it did on Thérèse. She describes a veil of faith as being "a wall that reaches all the way to the heavens." It is the ultimate trial. She further points out "When I sing of the eternal possession of God, I feel no happiness, because I sing only what I want to believe" (Ms C, 7v), and "My thoughts of Heaven [are no more] than cause for struggle and torment...a dismal tunnel" (Ms C, 5v).

The wall of darkness of faith can only fall down on the day of our entry into God's life. Thérèse says: "The first day of our final, eternal communion in heaven will be a day without a sunset" (Ms A, 35v–36r). Then, on the day when we enter God's life, we will discover that God is light, in him there is no darkness. It will be an eternal day, in eternal light, in a limitless bounty of love.

REFLECTION QUESTIONS

When faced with darkness do you gently turn to the Lord expecting his light? Can you recall a time in your journey when you were called beyond the blackness? What were the recognizable signs of the Lord's presence and support? What were the signs that were difficult to recognize?

DAY NINE

Storm of Suffering, Breath of Love

FOCUS POINT

Experience is the great teacher but it is inexperience that often precedes the teaching moment and which frames the challenge. To try and lead before full awareness and understanding is achieved is unwise and is often the root of our anxiety and our suffering.

I am not surprised you understand nothing that is going on in your soul. Could a small child, alone in a dinghy, lost on the stormy sea, know how far he is from shore? When he can still see the village from whence he has left, he knows how far he has traveled. When he notices the shore getting farther and farther away, he cannot contain his childlike joy. Oh, he says, the end of my voyage is near. But, as the beach gets farther away, the sea also appears to be bigger. Then the little child's knowledge is reduced to naught; he doesn't know where his craft is going anymore and, not knowing how to steer it, all he can do is surrender his sail to the whimsical wind....My Céline, Jesus' little child, is all alone in a dinghy. The shore is out of sight and she doesn't know where she is headed, whether she is moving forward or in reverse....Little Thérèse knows all too well; she is sure that her Céline is far asea and her small craft is sailing at full sail toward the harbor. But the rudder that Céline cannot see anymore is not unattended. Jesus is there, asleep, as he once was in the fishermen's boat on the sea of Galilee. He sleeps...and Céline does not see him, for night has descended upon the craft....Céline does not hear Jesus' voice. She hears the wind blowing and sees the darkness...and Jesus still sleeps. If only he would wake up for an instant, he could simply give a command to the wind and the sea, and there would be calm. The night would become brighter than day; Céline would see Jesus' divine glance and her soul would be comforted.

But, on the other hand, Jesus would not sleep anymore and he is so tired! His divine feet are tired from his pursuit of sinners; and he is resting so peacefully in Céline's little dinghy. The Gospels tell us that the apostles had given him a pillow, but in his beloved spouse's little dinghy, our Lord finds another, much softer, pillow. It is Céline's heart. There, he can leave everything behind; he is home. His head is not resting on a stone (like the stone he would complain about during his mortal life); it is resting on the heart of a child, a spouse. Oh how Jesus is happy! But how can he be happy when his spouse is suffering, when she is on watch, while he sleeps so peacefully? Does he not know that Céline sees only the night, that his divine face is hidden from her, and that the heaviness she feels in her heart is so hard for her to bear?

What a mystery! Jesus, the little baby from Bethlehem, whom Mary carried like "a light burden," is making himself so heavy, so heavy that even Saint Christopher is surprised by it....The wife from the sacred canticles also said that "her beloved is a bouquet of myrrh and he is resting on her breast." The myrrh is a symbol of suffering, and that is how Jesus is resting in Céline's heart....Nevertheless, Jesus is happy to see her suffer. He is happy to receive all that he needs from her throughout the night....He is waiting for dawn and then, oh then, what an awakening he will have!

So, be assured, my darling Céline, that even though your dinghy is far asea, it is perhaps already very close to your harbor. The wind of suffering that is propelling it is a wind of love and that wind is faster than lightning.

Thérèse of Lisieux, LT 144

What a difference there is between a storm and a breath! A storm destroys, while a breath restores life, but they are both a given on the road we have to travel.

At times, we find ourselves out on a sea of suffering; we are lost. The shore is so far away and the waves of suffering are so strong. There is no one there to save us. We don't know how to steer our craft back onto the right course to our destination; we are all alone, like a small child. It is then time for us to hear the Lord: "Do not, therefore, abandon that confidence of yours; it brings a great reward" (Heb 10:35). It is only when the storm has passed that we can see the breath, the light breeze, and then we understand with Thérèse: "Life is your vessel, not your dwelling...those words gave me courage and helped [my soul] endure exile" (Ms A, 41r).

These are words which help us wait until life's storms pass so that we can experience the breath of love. As long as the shore can be seen, we feel secure, and sailing our craft seems simple. But the farther we go from shore, the more we feel alone, at sea, without a true point of reference.

Suffering eliminates all points of reference and isolates us. With isolation, the burden becomes even heavier. Our child-like knowledge is skimpy and does not allow us to weather the storm. It is a time of profound confusion. We no longer feel the breath of love enveloping us. We are closed off and get nowhere. It is futile to act brave; that makes the danger even greater. Suffering always crushes.

Perhaps it is worth more to sit back and search the sky to try to find that little ray of light which will restore our courage. Thérèse describes it thus: "When dark clouds come to hide the Star of Love, the small bird doesn't move because he knows that the Sun still shines behind those clouds and that its true brightness will not be overshadowed for one single moment" (Ms B, 5r). It is called the Star of Love, because the Lord himself was tested by what he suffered, "he is able to help those who are being tested" (Heb 2:18); but he will always stay invigorated by the breath of love, the breath of the Spirit of love.

On the sea of life, our suffering along the road may, at times, shake us violently to the point at which we can only see the dark clouds, the harsh difficulties along the way, when nothing pierces the clouds. Thérèse remarks: "Sometimes, the little bird's heart finds itself bombarded by the storm. It seems to believe that nothing exists except the clouds surrounding it" (Ms B, 5r). Who hasn't had this happen to them? All horizons seem blocked, even the breath of love no longer invigorates anything. Since no end is in sight, it is time to surrender to the will of the wind, to prepare ourselves for the moment the storm will hit. If our own faith is a prisoner of those great clouds of suffering, how can it open itself to the light again?

Could it be that the Lord's word is not deeply enough embedded in us? These words should echo loudly in our ears: "My child, when you come to serve the Lord, prepare yourself for testing. Set your heart right and be steadfast, and do not be impetuous in time of calamity" (Sir 2:1–2). What a shame it would be to lose our footing along the road. Thérèse advises that "when we want to succeed, we must take the means to do so. Jesus made me understand that it was by the Cross that he wanted to give me souls" (Ms A, 69v).

The Cross was the road of Our Lord Jesus. His suffering was for love—a misunderstood, rejected, and scorned love. He didn't seek the suffering of the Cross; he didn't let the Cross stop him, he carried it of his own free will. He offered it through the inner breath of love. "Christ also suffered for you, leaving you an example…in his body, so that…we might live for righteousness" (1 Pet 2:21, 24).

Must we bear the crosses of suffering before carrying them in peace, that is to say, as an offering—an act which would change its meaning? We will always feel that we are weak little creatures. Thérèse says: "What happiness for it [the weak little creature] to stay there all the same, to try to find the invisible light which hides from its faith" (Ms B, 5r). There is neither stoicism nor masochism in this. Thérèse did not worship suffering any more than we do. She suffered a great deal; she suffered in sadness but she enlightens us with these words: "But, that is not how I suffer now. I suffer in joy and peace. I am truly happy to suffer" (Ms C, 4v). She was happy to suffer, not in a human way, but because Jesus made her understand the meaning of suffering, which can only be discovered through the gift of love.

Those who love are called to suffer because there is no love without suffering. It is the breath of humility which, nevertheless, maintains the love of those who suffer. And if the storm is only external, do not let it inside of ourselves. Thérèse says: "I fix it so that even in the midst of a storm, I keep calm inside" (DE 18.4.1). A storm on the inside is worse than a storm on the outside.

If fear takes over, and if suffering, with its crushing weight, defeats us, would we have not forgotten the passenger who steers with us? He sleeps, this Jesus, our traveling companion. He hears neither our cries for help nor the storm. Why are you sleeping, Lord? It's not the time for that. Make all our storms stop. But no, he still sleeps. He is too tired to notice that we are steering our craft as if he is not with us.

If he is still asleep, is it not because we aren't awakened in love? Does the breath of love invigorate us so little? If he sleeps, perhaps it is just the opposite; he is happy with "our childlike heart," a heart he loves in spite of the suffering, in spite of the difficult vigil before the battle, in spite of the stormy night amid the waves when all human horizons are blocked.

For those who can fight no longer and abandon the vigil, for those who can no longer detect the hidden presence of Jesus, only the night remains. For those who refused the breath of love, only the night remains. But those who keep their eyes on Jesus, the perfecter of our faith, will run the race with perseverance.

May Jesus, in his heart, make the wind of love, that breeze as light as a whisper, yet so powerful, steer us to the harbor without mishap. Love received from you, Lord, love lived for you is a breath of love in the hearts of the little children who we are. Your breath you gave back to the Father on the Cross, Jesus, so that it would invigorate us and make us withstand all of the storms of our life. When you will have silenced all our storms, then we will hear your whisper of love. Thérèse pledged: "Only love can buy love and as I searched, I found the way to soothe my heart is by giving you my love for your Divine Love" (Ms B, 4r).

REFLECTION QUESTIONS

Can you recall moments of suffering in your journey? Can you identify the feelings, thoughts, and emotions that were part of this experience? What was your reaction to Thérèse's assertion that "suffering produces isolation"? Can you recall being freed from your suffering by the activity of the Lord? What was necessary, what needed to change before the Lord was able to act on your behalf?

DAY TEN
A "Little Way"

FOCUS POINT

The Little Way presumes a childlike attitude toward life. It presumes awareness of who we are before God. The Little Way invites us to "unlearn" many of our supposedly mature and adult ways of looking at the world and learn the new ways of childlike dependence.

Yes, all goes well when we only seek the will of Jesus. This is why I, a poor little flower, am obedient to Jesus by trying to please my beloved Mother Superior.

Mother, as you well know, I have always wanted to be a saint. But, alas, I realized when I compared myself to the saints, that the difference between us was as great as the difference between a mountain peak, hidden by clouds, and a single grain of sand, under the feet of those passing by. Instead of being discouraged, I told myself: the Lord would not inspire unachievable desires.

Therefore, I can aspire to sainthood in spite of my small-ness. It is impossible for me to see myself greater than I am because I must see myself as I am, with all my imperfections. But I want to find the way to go to heaven by a direct route, one that is as short as possible, a totally new route.

We are in an era of inventions. For example, these days, one doesn't have to bother to climb stairs because the wealthy have elevators to easily replace them. Me, I would like to find an elevator to lift myself all the way up to Jesus, because I am too small to climb the harsh staircase of perfection. I searched all the holy books to find an indication of the elevator, the object of my desire. I read these words which came from the mouth of Eternal Wisdom: "If someone is very small, let him come to me." Then I came, discovering I had found what I was searching for. My Lord, I want to know! What would you do to the little one who could answer your call-ing?

I continued my search and this is what I found: "Like a mother caresses her child, this is how I will comfort you. I will carry you close to my breast and rock you on my lap!" Oh, never have there been more tender or melodious words to rejoice my soul. Jesus, your arms are the elevator which will lift me up to heaven! To achieve this, I must not grow; just the opposite, I must remain small. I must become smaller and smaller. Oh Lord, you have gone far beyond my expec-tations, and I want to sing of your mercies.

"O God, from my youth you have taught me, and I still proclaim your wondrous deeds, so even to old age I will pro-claim your might to all the generations to come" (Ps 71:17–18). What will this old age be for me? It seems to me that it could be now because in the eyes of the Lord, two thousand years is no more than twenty years...than a single day....

Beloved Mother, don't think that your child wants to leave you now....Don't believe that she puts a higher value on dying at dawn rather than at dusk. She only wants to please Jesus....Now, as he seems to be approaching her to draw her to her time of glory, your child rejoices. For a long time, she has understood that God needs no one, her even less than others, to do good on earth.

Thérèse of Lisieux, Ms C, 2v–3r–3v

For a long time, the God of the Christians appeared to be a distant God, unapproachable, the God of fear and dread. How could we have recognized him as a God of love, like a Father, full of tenderness? And despite our perception of God as vengeful, he still calls us to sainthood and opens his kingdom of glory to each one of us.

Thérèse, who assumed the way of spiritual childhood, shed some light on this for us, reminding us that the path of spiritual childhood is a road of trust and surrender which carries us on the way. Her goal was this: "I want to teach souls about the small ways that have worked for me, to tell them that there is just one thing to do here below on earth: shower Jesus with the flowers of their small sacrifices" (DE 17.7.2). Confidence, self-abandonment, offerings: these are the characteristics of the road that the Lord teaches to the humble, the road of the will of God which he puts in our whole heart. Isn't this the same road the Son took to the Father—the Son who continuously achieved the will of the Father and who gave himself to him in self-abandonment and love at the time of his supreme offering on the Cross? Is this not the road of all saintliness?

Is it possible that sainthood has been presented to us as a result of his victories and not through his battles and loving responses? Or, maybe it is all of it! The grandeur of sainthood reveals itself according to the degree of love. Be we mountain or single grain of sand, it doesn't matter as long as we have responded to divine love with our own love. The little one is also called to sainthood, for even frailty provokes the loving support of the God of love.

The Lord is at our side and reminds us: "Walk before me, and be blameless" (Gen 17:1) and "Follow me" (Mt 9:9). My imperfections are there; even if they slow my pace on the road, they will not stop my advance, because "the Light of the world" (Jn 8:12) is there. He shows us the way.

Our road is a new one, very short and straight. How can we understand? Will all of the obstacles instantly disappear as I ascend? One must be careful not to take the road of empty dreams and utopian promises.

The little way is only for the very small. It is not for those who draw their support from their own strength and knowledge of the road, but it is for those who draw support from the strength of the Lord and his comforting presence. The road is short because it is a straight road. Only those who are small will allow themselves to be carried by the One who arose from earth to heaven in the splendor and triumph of his Resurrection.

How can a little one, who is so weak, possibly withstand the rough road to perfection? Fascinated by the Divine Eagle, the arisen Jesus, he lets himself be borne on eagles' wings (Ex 19:4) to reach the summit of love. It is a little way, brand new and in a constant state of renewal, because it requires us to divest ourselves of all old, worn ideas, certainties, and assurances so that we can enter into the eternal newness of Christ, into his eternal youth and allow ourselves to be reclothed by him with the strength, grace, and the always new love of God.

The direct little way of love is only for the little ones, "My path is all trust and all love," says Thérèse. "I see that it is enough to recognize one's nothingness and to give oneself up, like a child, to the arms of God" (LT 226). It is not as simple as it seems for us who think that we are grown up, wise, and experienced. If it was that way, we should take the elevator. Even to pull oneself up to the wings of the Divine Eagle, we need help, just like a child needs help to climb up to his father's back. Even without words, with uplifted arms, and an imploring glance, the little one is understood. This is the way in which we must humbly and simply give ourselves up to God's hands, and repeat to ourselves in the words of Thérèse: "I am this child, object of the provident love of the Father" (Ms A, 39r).

As the Father loves Jesus, he, in turn, loves us and draws us toward the Father. Jesus is "the way, and the truth, and the life" (Jn 14:6), and the only way to the Father. If the little one goes through Jesus, it is really to join the Father, just as all children go toward their fathers. They go not to a Father who is angry, vindictive, vengeful, weak, and insignificant, but to a Father who is all love, who wraps each child with his tenderness, revealing his love and calling them to love him.

It is a little way of love which leads to the Father because the Father "did not send his Son to redeem the righteous, but the sinners" (Ms A, 39r). He sent his Son to free each of us from our imperfections, our folly of greatness, and to lead us to love like a small child, to lead us to know we are loved because we are so small. Isn't it true that a small child will not open his arms or smile at someone unless he feels love through open arms, a peaceful face, or a loving smile?

This is the little way that the Lord reveals to whoever searches for it in truth: the face of the Father who is full of tenderness, who reveals his love to his child, who offers consolation in difficult times, who carries the child when the road becomes too rocky, who shares his delights and joys. It is the face of our Father in heaven who, by revealing the love of the Father, opens us up to love. It is the true face of our God and Father, an eternal face of love, whom humankind, at various times in history, has disfigured past the point of recognition. It is a face that the little Thérèse would have given her life to have rehabilitated. It is the face that we can only discover through the Holy Face of Jesus; it is the Holy Face through which we reach the divine and blazing fire of the Blessed Trinity. The route is one of the self-abandonment of the little child "who sleeps without fear in his father's arms" (LT 196), because we can only sleep if we are at peace, breathing contentedly in an environment of love.

Don't even think about how far we could go on the path if we did not take an active role in the climb. Our love must answer God's love. But how? Thérèse tell us that Jesus doesn't ask for big deeds, but simply self-abandonment and gracious recognition. And again, as little children, we will testify to his love: "by not letting a single chance go by for a small sacrifice, not a glance, not a word, to take advantage of all the little things and to do them out of love" (Ms B, 4 r–v).

The little road, straight and new, is not bliss; but it takes us there. "Since I am a very small soul," avers Thérèse, "I work to please Jesus, to placate his whims" (CSG 57). It is good to take action in the freedom of love, like a small child, and like the small souls who run along the path of spiritual childhood, waiting to rejoice in their father's glorious home, introduced by the Divine Sun, inflamed by the fire of the spirit of love. This is the little way which leads to the vast horizons of the kingdom of glory.

REFLECTION QUESTIONS

Recall a past experience of dependency and identify that which you found appealing and that which you found unappealing. Recall an experience of independence and identify that which attracted you about the experience and that which you found unattractive. Compare and contrast the two experiences and discover the choices that need to be made in order to walk the path of the Little Way of Saint Thérèse.

The Word: A Presence to Cherish

FOCUS POINT

The Word is revealed to us in the worshiping community, in the Eucharist which is the most Blessed Sacrament of the Altar, and through the sacred Scriptures. The presence of the Word is intended to nourish us and to strengthen us for our journey.

This is the picture of our souls: often, we go down into the fertile valleys where our heart likes to feed, the great field of Scripture, which has so often opened up before us to spread out its vast treasures in our favor. To us, that great field now seems to be a dry, waterless desert....We don't even know where we are. Instead of peace and light, we find trouble, or at the least, darkness....But, just like the spouse, we know the reason for our trial.

We are not yet in our homeland (in heaven); and hardship is supposed to purify us, like gold in the crucible. We sometimes feel abandoned. Alas, are those chariots and vain noises which assail us coming from within or outside? We don't know, but Jesus does; he sees our sadness and then suddenly, his soothing voice echoes, softer than the breath of spring: "Return, return, O Shulammite! Return, return, that we may look upon you" (Song 6:13). What a call from our Spouse! ...Why not? We dared not look at ourselves because we felt we were plain and without luster, and now Jesus is calling us. He wants to gaze upon us at his leisure, but he is not alone. He comes with the other two persons of the Holy Trinity to take possession of our soul....

As Jesus promised, when he was about to return to his Father and our Father, he said, with great tenderness: "If someone loves me, he will keep my teachings and my Father will love him and we shall come to him and dwell within him." The only way to our happiness and proof of our love is to keep the word of Jesus. But what is his word?...It seems to me that Jesus is the word, himself....Jesus, himself, the word, the word of God!...He said it to us later in the Gospel of Saint John, while praying to his Father for the disciples. He said it this way: "Sanctify them in the truth; your word is truth" (Jn 17:17).

In another passage, Jesus taught us that he is the way, the truth, the life. From this we know what word we must follow; we do not have to ask Jesus, as Pilate did: "What is the truth?" We already have the truth within us; it is Jesus. We must keep Jesus in our hearts!

Thérèse of Lisieux, LT 165 to Céline

A mother waits for the first word from her little one who says it when he is able to identify the person who is in front of him; then it will be said all in one word: "Mama." It is most often the first word that comes from the mouth of a baby.

Speech is the expression of language for humankind. Jesus, the living word of God, was the one who came from the Father to tell us about God. "In the beginning was the Word, and the Word was with God, and the Word was God" (Jn 1:1). "God, in these last days, he has spoken to us by a Son" (Heb 1:2).

Jesus, the living word of God, whom we discover in the vast field of Scripture is even more evident in the Gospels, the Good News. Says Thérèse: "Above all, it is the Gospels which give me support for all my prayers. Through the word, all the needs of my poor soul are met" (Ms A, 83r). Each day of the year, the Church opens us to the Gospels, so that we can discover in them the treasures of life. There we are not served rewarmed leftovers, but a brand new meal each day. We must look to see, in the light of the Spirit, what word will reach us today, for as Thérèse remarks: "I have often noticed that Jesus doesn't come and stock me with provisions, he constantly provides me with new nourishment. I find it within me, without even knowing how it got there" (Ms A, 76v).

Those who look for God, seek a word, not to be gleaned by chance, but received in the Church of today, like a choice morsel. We may, perhaps, at times, find ourselves lost when faced with a well-known text which reveals nothing to us. We must go back and read and reread it again until that single word rises up into our heart, like a marvelous gift from God. "The word is very near to you; it is in your mouth and in your heart for you to observe" (Deut 30:14). This word is in our hearts, a pearl in its treasure chest; we must open the chest to discover the jewel. We must abandon our sense of self so that we can open ourselves to the gift of God, open ourselves to Jesus who is himself hidden in the bottom of the humble heart. Jesus is hidden because the "word was made flesh, and he dwells within us."

The darkness of discouragement, lack of understanding, giving up on the search, pretentiousness, and pride may close our hearts to the word. We must come to Jesus like a disciple; and the disciple will dwell in the word and know the "truth and the truth will make us free" (Jn 8:32).

It is in the Light of the word that each of us will be enlightened. We must be disciples and seekers of truth with a mind open to the meaning of the Scriptures and a heart open for love. We must become silent within ourselves because the Lord only comes in a whisper of love. He only comes when the noises of knowledge have stopped, and we dwell with Jesus, listening for his word. We must have a free, unencumbered heart to be able to respond and love.

A disciple's heart discovers the true face of the Master by means of his word and marvels at these hidden meanings until they proclaim themselves. The words are made flesh through us; Thérèse says: "I always discover new sources of light with hidden and mysterious meanings in the Gospels" (Ms A, 83v). But to discover this new source, we must look for it and then welcome it into ourselves, in the certainty that the word will change us. Without condemning those books which open us to knowledge, we must go back directly to the Gospels themselves, as Thérèse always returned to the living source: "For myself, I no longer find anything unless it is in the Gospels. That alone is enough for me" (DE 15.5.3). Why are the Gospels so significant? This is true because they are books of love, tenderness, life, and the light of God. The Gospels become books of conversion, loving responses. They reveal the footprints of Jesus on the path he took.

Is there a chance that we may become disillusioned? Is there a chance that we may lose our way? Not so, says Thérèse: "Since Jesus has returned to heaven, I can only follow him by the tracks he left, but these tracks are so bright and fragrant! I only have to direct my eyes to the holy Gospels and right away, I breathe in the perfume of the life of Jesus and I know which way to run" (Ms C, 36v).

Following in the footsteps of Jesus, we are sure to find our way, not in a dream, but through a profound faith in his words, as long as we dwell in his love. "Those who love me will keep my word, and my Father will love them, and we will come to them and make our home with them" (Jn 14:23).

In the silence of a heart that is inhabited by the Father and the Son, words of adoration and praise will pour forth, given life by the Holy Spirit. No spoken words are needed, for as Thérèse points out: "The Doctor of all doctors teaches without words....I have never heard him speak but I know he is inside me. At each and every moment of my life, he guides me to do what I must do. Just when I need it, I discover lights I have never seen before" (Ms A, 83v). There are no little voices on the little way of love, but there is the certainty of a loving presence in our hearts, like a herald of light, which helps us hear the call to the road, and follow the path.

The only condition for our happiness and the only proof of our love for Jesus is for us to keep the word of God. Keep the word and recite it every day so that it will penetrate our hearts and transform us. Keep the word like a flame of love which floods today with light. Keep the word, like a compass to guide us on the right course and like a star that leads us on the true path.

This word is not something inert that we keep to ourselves and jealously watch over. "The word of Jesus is Jesus himself." Jesus is the living word whose voice we become by our own lives. "Welcome with meekness the implanted word that has the power to save your souls" (Jas 1:21), which brings fruit through love. The word shapes us in the image of the Beloved so that we may become reflections of the Gospels, the Good News of the loving face of our Lord.

Jesus is in us, with the Father and the Holy Spirit who inflame our hearts. "Your words became to me a joy and the delight of my heart" (Jer 15:16). We must always turn inward to discover the loving presence and the word of truth which enlightens and frees us. Along the route, we must repeat to ourselves a motto of Thérèse: "Jesus does it all, I do nothing" (LT 142). Put no obstacles before Jesus; allow him to freely enter your heart. Vigilantly keep him in your heart, living off his loving presence. It is in this manner that one pursues the road of love, even when the path is sometimes difficult, right up until the Lord's final call beckons. "If anyone keeps his word, God's love is made complete in him" (1 Jn 2:5). At that point seeing myself in Jesus will be possible.

REFLECTION QUESTIONS

Is the word of God my lover, my friend, or a casual acquaintance? What are the choices that I need to make in order to be in a daily relationship with the Word? What other words do I listen to instead of listening to the word that comes from the Lord?

Prayer: A Missionary Apostolate

FOCUS POINT

The power of our prayer is a dynamic response to the call of our God to join in proclaiming the kingdom of God. Our prayer is not static but rather goes out from us, unites with the prayers of our brothers and sisters, and produces the fruit of the harvest.

I have recently had a thought that I must share with my Céline. One day, when I was thinking of things I could do to save souls, a story from the Gospels enlightened me. In that story, Jesus was showing his disciples some fields of ripe wheat when he said: "Lift up your eyes and see how the crops in the fields are ready for harvesting," and later, "Truly, the harvest is plentiful, but there are not enough workers. Ask the harvest master to send more workers." What a mystery!

Is Jesus not almighty? Do the creatures not belong to their creator? If so, then why does Jesus say to ask the harvest master to send more workers? Why?...Oh, he does it because he has so much love for us that he wants us to take part in the salvation of souls. He wants to do nothing without us. The creator of the universe awaits the prayer of a poor little soul to save other souls, redeemed like it, at the price of his blood.

Our apostolate is not to go harvest the ripe wheat in the field. Jesus does not tell us to look down at the fields and go harvest them; our mission is more sublime. Jesus told us to lift up our eyes and see. He tells us to see how many empty places there are in heaven and that it is up to us to fill them. He explains that we are his Moses, praying on the mountain. Ask him for more workers and he will send them; he is only waiting for a prayer, or even a sigh from our hearts!

Isn't the apostolate of prayer of more value than just simple words? Our mission as Carmelites is to train evangelical workers who will, in turn, save thousands of souls, of whom we will be the mothers....Céline, if those were not the words of our Lord, himself, who would ever believe them? I find our role to be a beautiful one; we have no need to envy the priests.

Thérèse of Lisieux, LT 235 to Céline

D o we pray or evangelize? That is the wrong question. Our posture must be to pray in order to evangelize; a prayer which comes from the true source—our Lord—sent out to the fields to be sown, cultivated, and harvested. As in any environment of growth, it is not necessarily the same people who tend to all its aspects from start to finish. Some can only draw from the source to give to others who benefit from it. No one can claim to harvest spiritually entirely on his or her own.

Prayer is always at the very core of the mission. The missionary prayer from each of us is the sole condition for there to be a mission. "You should represent the people before God and you should bring their cases before God" (Ex 18:19). That is our calling and our message, to stand before God, like supplicants, so that everyone is represented before him. What a wonderful job we have, to call God's attention to his children and raise them up to him!

Our prayers must be humble: "Let the words of my mouth and the meditation of my heart be acceptable to you, O LORD, my rock and my redeemer" (Ps 19:14). Prayers may be cries and pleas, but they may also be strong internal surges, which are the work of the Spirit of Love, which are nothing more than mere sighs. For Thérèse the form that prayer took was not a cause for concern: "For me, prayer is a burst from my heart. It is a simple glance thrown towards Heaven, a cry of thanksgiving and love in times of trial, as well as in times of joy. Finally, it is something big, supernatural, which opens up my soul and unites me with Jesus" (Ms C, 25r–v).

Prayer is all of these things: a surge, a glance, a cry, a loving response, a time of contemplation, a physical or moral hardship. Whether the prayer comes from us or from others, whether it is for ourselves or others, it does not divide. Prayer is a profound and mysterious form of unity, as Thérèse explains: "Do you know what gives me strength? Well, I do all my work and dedicate it to a missionary. When I think that one of them, far away, is exhausted from his apostolic duties, I offer my own fatigue to God to reduce his" (DE 228). After this, who could still claim that prayer is just an escape, a refuge? No, prayer is the link with apostolic action. It is the projection of the source upon the witnesses of the Gospel. Without prayer, the mission could be solely a human act. Nevertheless, we are God's messengers. Nothing is achieved without his gift, the gift of his blessing.

Sometimes our view of the Church and the world is hazy. We do not see the fields to be harvested because we expect something else. We have our own projects, but God presents us with his own priorities: "Lift up your eyes and see." We must do the Father's work, not our own. Often, we can only see the fruits of grace in the eye's of God's children through hope and faith. That is some vision.

Who knows whether or not there are enough workers? We each have our own ideas about the conditions under which apostolic workers are chosen, as if the choice was up to us! Such is not the word of Jesus. He asks us to pray to the harvest master, God, to send workers for his harvest. He calls the workers, he chooses, and sends them: he, not us! We only ask that he send some; the prerequisites for choosing them are not our concern. That is for the master himself. What the Father expects from us is a prayer of servitude, like a child: "Ask and it will be given you" (Lk 11:9) and "Ask and you will receive, so that your joy may be complete" (Jn 16:24). Our plea must be one of faith. Like beggars we must hope to be heard. Perhaps we will first have to say: "Lord, teach us to pray" (Lk 11:1) so that we may really understand the missionary place of our prayers in the life of the Church.

Have we given sufficient thought to this request that the Lord awaits from us? He invites us to ask because he wants to share his work with us. He wants to do nothing without us. And now, we would want to do something without him! That is impossible in spiritual works.

Proclaims Thérèse: "How great is the power of prayer!…It isn't necessary to read a nice formula from a book for a particular circumstance for a prayer to be granted. If it was so… alas, how I should be pitied!" (Ms C, 25r). Sometimes, ready-made formulas for prayers are useful to get us started. We can gather them along the way. Familiarity with the word of God should already dwell in our hearts to the point that we can recite his own words to him by means of the Psalms: cries of adoration, praise, supplication, and suffering. At times, it will make us sing like the harvester tying up the bundles. In the end, our prayer bursts forth from our heart to reach God's heart.

There is the sower, and there is the harvester. There are a variety of jobs in the Lord's fields. Others include the one who restores courage, and the one who stores the harvest. Not everyone is used at harvest time. Have we thought about the length of time between the sowing of the seed and the harvest, and about all our questions regarding hope for the future?

It is a time to live through prayer for those whose mission is to become an apostle, people such as small children, youth in search of a future, monks, friars, and sisters in the silence of cloisters, parents, the ill, and those for whom age presents a handicap.

We are all alone in our prayers, before our Lord to ask him: "Give heed to me, O Lord…[and] remember how I stood before you" (Jer 18:19–20). Each of us should say, along with Thérèse, from the bottom of our hearts: "I feel a great desire to work at converting sinners" (Ms A, 45v). The Lord has told us to lift up our eyes. We must leave the earthly harvest, crying out to the heavens and lifting up our glance toward the only One who will send those workers who await his call with a free and loving heart.

God's work can only be achieved in communion with him, supported by his presence, and by the gift of his grace. Only prayer opens heaven to us. Thérèse declares: "The Almighty gave the saints a solid foundation to lean on: himself and only him; and as a lever: he gave us prayer, which ignites with a fire of love. That is how the saints who are still active excite the world and how, until the end of time, the saints to come will also do it" (Ms C, 36v). Without the lever of prayer, the mission will stagnate. Through the prayers of each of us, evangelical workers will seed and reap the Lord's harvest.

Each of us receives our portion of the mission in the Church, and no one may give it to another. Each of us has our own job to do. Because it is better to talk to God than to talk about God, each evangelical worker, following Jesus' example, will always begin by speaking to the Lord in the silence of his or her heart. Only then will the workers be able to call God by his name.

REFLECTION QUESTIONS

In what way do you recognize your prayer as a powerful tool the Lord uses for evangelization? In those moments when you feel alone and your prayer lifeless, what do you need to help you see that your effort and response is not in vain? Do you reserve time each day in your prayer to listen to the Lord, assuming the posture of the obedient helper, so that your prayer may be the response that the Lord prefers?

DAY THIRTEEN
The Vocation of Love

When people are in love their hearts sing. All seems possible, every experience imagined seems within their grasp, and it is believed that the only requirement is to choose from the bounty before them in order to be nourished and filled. Nothing seems too much or unattainable.

Oh Jesus, to be your bride, to be a Carmelite, to become the mother of all souls through my union with you that should satisfy me....However, such is not the case....Without a doubt, these three privileges are my vocation: Carmelite, bride, and mother....Yet, within me, I feel the need for other vocations. I feel called to the vocation of warrior, of priest, of apostle, of doctor, of martyr; finally, I feel the need, the desire to do it all for you, Jesus, all of the most heroic tasks....In my soul I feel the courage of a Crusader, of a Pontifical [Soldier]. I would like to die on a battlefield, defending the Church.

I feel that, within me, I have the vocation to be a priest. How lovingly, Jesus, I would hold you in my hands, when at the sound of my voice, you would come down from heaven into the Eucharist....It is with such love, I would give you to the souls....But, alas, while I desire to be a priest, I admire and yearn for the humbleness of Saint Francis of Assisi. I feel the vocation to do as he did by refusing the sublime dignity of the priesthood. Oh Jesus, my love, my life...how can I reconcile these contrasts? How can I achieve the desires of my poor little soul?

In spite of my humbleness, I would like to enlighten other souls as the prophets and the Doctors of the Church did. My vocation is to be an apostle....I want to travel the earth and preach your name and plant your cross on unfaithful soil. However, my Beloved, I will not be satisfied to do just one mission. At the same time, I would like to proclaim your Gospel to all the corners of the earth, even to the most se- cluded places....

I want to be a missionary, not just for a few years, but to have been one from the creation of the world and be one up until the end of all time....But above all, my Savior, I want to shed my blood for you, right to the very last drop....

Martyrdom, that is my childhood dream. That dream has grown with me in the cloisters of Carmel.... But there again I feel that my dream is a fantasy, because I could not limit myself to want just one type of martyrdom....For me to be satisfied, I would need to experience them all....Like you, my beloved husband, I want to be whipped and crucified....I would like to die, stripped bare, like Saint Bartholomew.... Like Saint John, I want to be plunged into boiling oil. I would like to submit to all of the tortures inflicted upon the mar- tyrs....With Saint Agnes and Saint Cecilia, I would present my neck to the blade of the sword. And, like my dear sister, Joan of Arc, I would like to whisper your name while I am tied to the burning stake....Oh Jesus...just by thinking about the torments which will be the lot of Christians in the time of the anti-Christ, I feel my heart quiver. I want to reserve all these torments for myself....

Jesus, if I would like to write down all of my desires, I would have to borrow your book of life. Recorded there are the deeds of all the saints. These are the things I would have liked to have accomplished for you....Oh Jesus, what will your response be to all my fantasies?

Thérèse of Lisieux, Ms B, 2v–3r

On Easter night, we sing of Mother Church and proclaim "all my springs are in you" (Ps 87:7). Thérèse exclaims: "The Church, my mother!" Are we dreaming? No, we're not. Vatican II tells us that the Church is "our mother, the spouse without sin of the Lamb without sin, the Body of Christ"; and that we, "through the diversity of its members and functions, are one body, renewed by the one Spirit, and called to sainthood, the fruit of the grace of the Holy Spirit."

Take a look at the Church which has carried us through the conflicts which have arisen from time to time. We look in a glance of humility because we are sinners in the holy Church. It is a look of truth; but it is also a look of love, for as Thérèse often repeats: "My Jesus, I love you. I love the Church, my mother" (Ms B, 4v).

This is what opens my horizons for service in and for the Church. I draw life for my inner self from the Church. I serve through the humility of my heart for the Body of Christ which

is the Church. We can only serve by offering ourselves to
love—otherwise, it would be pride, domination, fruitless criti-
cism, and failure. The ecclesiastical body can only live in a
communion woven with Christ. We must work to find our
place to serve in the Church so we can fill our service with
love. Thérèse explains: "I understood that if the Church had
a body…it also had a heart and this heart was burning with
love. (…) Yes, I found my place in the Church and this place,
Lord, you have given to me….In the heart of the Church, my
mother, I will be love….In this way, I will be everything" (Ms
B, 3v).

All manner of missionary callings could be born from a
free and generous heart, even if they don't all come to frui-
tion—a warrior to fight against the forces of evil which could
hurt humankind; a priest to offer, serve, and deliver oneself
to love so that life can appear; an apostle to carry the light of
the Gospels to all places; a doctor to loudly proclaim the
truth in the midst of the invasive noises of the world; a martyr to give testimony each day to the faith that lights the way;
a crusader to defend the Church's interests to the point of
giving one's life on the battlefield. Isn't it true that we always
lose some part of ourselves in every form of a vocational call?

Why not become a priest when we have recognized love?
"He [Jesus] laid down his life for us—and we ought to lay
down our lives for one another" (1 Jn 3:16). Those words
are not laying a claim to a vocation. More precisely, they
signify the discovery of the grace we have been given through
the ones who are called into love's service and offer themselves to love. We give our hands, our voices, our very lives to
Christ in loving service by allowing ourselves to be taken over
completely by him, by baring ourselves, following the example of Jesus, God's humble servant.

How can we be everything if we are so small? Thérèse answers: "I understood that love encompasses all vocations and that love is everything. Love encompasses all times and places. In a word, it is eternal! Then, in the overabundance of my extraordinary love, I exclaimed: Jesus, my love...my vocation, I finally found my vocation, it is Love!" (Ms B, 3v). Those words: What a large task they represent! We must understand and grasp the meaning, turn it inward and then act upon it. We must understand that love is everything, no matter what vocation it brings. In order to do that, we must have known and believed the love God has for us, because "God is love, and those who abide in love abide in God, and God abides in them" (1 Jn 4:16). Love is received first, before it is lived.

Love is the fire that powers our actions. "For love is strong as death...it burns like a blazing fire, it blazes like a mighty flame" (Song 8:6). The love of God abides in us and transforms us. It is the fire of love which endlessly invigorates our love, so it will never wane, as Thérèse reminds us: "I understood that only love made the members of the Church act. If love died, the apostles would no longer proclaim the Good News and the martyrs would refuse to shed their blood" (Ms B, 3v). If it appears to us, at times, that God's servants seem discouraged, lack dynamism, or even if there are fewer workers to harvest love, could it be because the fire of love has cooled in their hearts? Never let the fire of love go out!

We must offer ourselves to the life-giving breath of the Holy Spirit to rekindle our apostolic ardor. Thérèse points out that "the smallest act of pure love is more useful to the Church than all other deeds put together" (Ms B, 4v). How beautiful this deep conviction is! But, we cannot evade the question of ourselves: Is pure love really in our hearts? Do we act for ourselves or for the Lord? Do we wait for the glory or do we take refuge in humble service? Do we work half-heartedly or in generous availability and selflessness? These questions deserve a true answer; we must stop and think about them. It is not just any love that dwells in us: "Righteous Father....so that the love with which you have loved me may be in them" (Jn 17:25, 26). It is a loving gift which is gathered like a sacrificial offering and then scattered over all God's children. In this way, our love is your love, and your love is the totality of you, Lord. Then, by participating in your totality, our own love will become our entire being, everything in our lives.

We must be as the little soul who would like to be all love for our Lord who is all love. We must go toward those who misunderstand love, here and far away, and give of ourselves to the very limits of love. We must act as great witnesses of love, to live all manner of self-disclosure, humiliation, and torture. We must struggle to recognize all of the various forms of suffering and trials along our path to the Lord. Without love, we do not move from wishful thinking to purposeful desire. Lord, are the stories in your book of life—the saintly faces of the multitudes that surrounds you—not a reflection of the totality of love in the humble human condition?

Thérèse asks how an imperfect soul such as hers could hope to have the fulfillment of divine love. She tells us that she would take over God's burning love for herself and learn "the sublime song of love" from the Lord. A simple whisper will become a song, in the humility of all the love lived in the Church, our mother, when our entire being becomes an echo of God's love, thanks to the Holy Spirit who granted us our capacity to love. Does this seem foolish to the world? Without a doubt for some, but not to you, O Lord. Wasn't it you who taught us that song of love? Wasn't it you who never stopped saying to us: "I love you"?

REFLECTION QUESTIONS

Recall your own experience of being in love. Can you remember what you were feeling and your attitude toward life and the choices ahead? Which of these feelings, hopes, and desires are still with you today? Are any of these same feelings present in your developing relationship with the Lord? Are there any hopes and desires that you wish to bring to your prayer this day?

The Infinite Horizons of the Lord's Justice and Mercy

FOCUS POINT

Every person readily calls to mind a distinct and unique picture of God when they begin to reflect on God's justice and mercy. Our image of God is informative of who we are as a person in relationship to the Father, Son, and Spirit.

I know that one must be very pure to appear before the God of all holiness, but I also know that the Lord is infinitely just. It is this justice—a justice that seems to frighten so many souls—that is the object of my joy and confidence. To be just is not only to be strict in punishing the guilty; it is also to recognize righteous intentions and reward virtue. I expect as much from God's justice as from his mercy. Because he is just, he is compassionate and filled with tenderness, slow to punish and generous with mercy. Because he knows our frailty, he remembers that we are only dust. The Lord has compassion for us in the same way as a father has tenderness for his children. That, my brother, is what I think about the justice of our Lord. My path is all trust and love. I don't understand the souls who are afraid of such a tender friend.

Sometimes, when I read a certain spiritual book, where perfection is shown in the midst of a thousand obstacles, surrounded by so many illusions, my poor little mind tires very quickly. I close that learned book which strains my mind and dries up my heart and reach for the Holy Bible. Then, all seems bright. A single passage opens my soul to the discovery of infinite horizons; and perfection appears simple to me. I see that it is enough for us just to recognize our nothingness and to give ourselves up, like a child, to the arms of God.

Leaving the study of these great books, which I can't understand, let alone put into practice, to the great souls and learned spirits, I can rejoice in being small since I know that only children and those who seem small will be admitted to the heavenly banquet. I am so happy that there are many rooms in the kingdom of God because if there was only the one I read about, I could not even think of entering it, as that room and the road to it are incomprehensible to me.

However, I don't want to be too far from your home. Considering your qualities, I hope that God will give me the grace to participate in your glory here on earth, just as would the sister of a conqueror, even if she is devoid of the gifts of nature. She wants to participate, in spite of her poverty, in the honor given to her brother.

Thérèse of Lisieux, LT 226 to Father Roulland

The little way is straight because it is a road of mercy and justice. But why have we disfigured the face of the Father so often? To some people, God seems to be uncompromising and heartless, a God who traps humankind. We forget the God of tenderness who forgives and has mercy. Admittedly, each of God's children is asked to give an explanation of their life story so that they can, before his loving face, retell their own life works. But this recitation is done within the realm of God's own interpretation of it, laden with the love God gives us at that time. It is not certain that we will always understand his mercy. This is not an invitation to let everything go simply because that action would not be one of love.

"From the fullness of Jesus, we have all received, grace upon grace" (Jn 1:16) because "God so loved the world that he gave his only Son, so that everyone who believes in him may not perish but may have eternal life" (Jn 3:16). The Son was given to the world "in order that the world might be saved through him" (Jn 3:17). That is what we should be filled with: the gift of life, the gift of love from God so that we will always live through him.

Yes, the Lord is totally just in the infiniteness of his being, but his justice is unfailingly tied to his mercy. It is true, he shows people their responsibilities because he respects their freedom to say "yes" or "no" to them. But, at the same time, he can, in truth, read the deepest intentions of his children's hearts and reveal the good which has been achieved. God is just because he is the truth. Because he is just, he is merciful. Thérèse reminds us: "God gave me his infinite mercy, and through it, I gaze upon and adore the other divine perfections! Then, they all appear to be shining with love; even justice appears to be cloaked with love" (Ms A, 83v). Even if we stray in our false conceptions about God's justice and think that he will make us pay dearly, guilty as we are, God's mercy is still filled with love.

On the Cross, Jesus gave to the ultimate limit so that the debt of all humankind could be forgiven. It is a pressing call for each of us to let ourselves be forgiven and restored through love. Exclaims Thérèse: "What sweet happiness to think that God is just! That is to say, he takes into account our weaknesses and he knows full well of the fragility of our nature" (Ms A, 83v). Before God, we are nothing more than small grains of dust. He doesn't brush us away with a flick of his hand; he gazes lovingly upon us and his gaze changes the grain of sand into a shining grain of love. Then, the Lord can say: "And I will take you for my wife; I will take you for my wife in righteousness and in justice, in steadfast love, and in mercy. I will take you for my wife in faithfulness" (Hos 2:19–20).

The little way is not a road of fear and dread, but a path of confidence and love, for love casts out fear. "The Father wants me to love him," says Thérèse, "because he has given me not just a great deal, but all. He does not wait for me to love him...but he wanted me to know that he had given me his inexplicable provident love, so that now, I am deeply in love with him" (Ms A, 39r). In fact, those who fear God's justice look at themselves in negative ways, whereas those who believe in mercy, read their own positive side in God. But to believe in mercy, we must know within ourselves that we are loved by God to the limit and must respond to his love to the limit of our own ability to love.

There are still certain spiritual writers in existence who depict the devil extending his hand to the masses as if he were going to do some good. Conversely, there are others who ignore the devil as if he was no longer present along our path. We must make sure that it isn't the devil who leads us along our path; we must follow God's lead, walk in his footprints.

The way to fight against the devil is given to us in the book of the word of God and in the book of life where the story of God's witnesses is written. And beyond this technique, we must first read about the infinite horizons that God's merciful love opens to us. These beautiful, knowledgeable books are far from being useless. They facilitate our way and pave our path to more extensive reading.

Yet, the little ones who follow the little way do not see as far ahead as that. They cannot reason for themselves. More simply, they bathe themselves in the rays of love which the God of love sends them. The little ones are never deprived of light or grace. Didn't Jesus say: "Let the little children come to me...for it is to such as these that the kingdom of God belongs" (Lk 18:16)? The Lord can make his mercy shine only into the lives of those who have made themselves small, for as Thérèse remarks: "Because I was humble and weak, he came down to me and secretly instructed me in the ways of his love" (Ms A, 49r). How can we fear a God who comes down to our level, who, through Jesus, made himself human, to seek out and save the lost? How can we not let our hearts be touched by God, the God of tenderness and faithfulness, mercy and forgiveness, the God whose mercy extends from one generation to the next?

If we happen to find that we have strayed far afield, we must not stop along the route. We must continue until we accept our weakness. Cautions Thérèse: "Jesus, I can't begin to tell the little souls just how beyond words your condescension is....As impossible as it seems, I feel that if you should find a weaker soul than mine, you would happily give it larger favors, if it gave itself in total confidence to your infinite mercy" (Ms B, 5v). It is all there, in the abandonment of the self, in the giving over of ourselves to God's mercy; it is not gained by sadly looking at our limitations and poverty, for that negativity locks us up inside of ourselves.

"Your merciful love," assures Thérèse, "yearns to set souls ablaze" (Ms A, 84r). Let this fire of mercy consume our faults so that we will arise, standing in the light, because we are made for the light and for life. Jesus comes so that we might have abundant life, the life in the kingdom to come, in the kingdom of God's light where he reveals his justice and mercy to us. With this coming also comes a sense of certainty and security that arises out of Jesus' presence.

The Gospel says: "Father, I desire that those whom you have given me may be with me where I am, to see my glory" (Jn 17:24), and "In my Father's house, there are many rooms" (Jn 14:2). There are as many rooms as there are joys of love in his children's hearts. These rooms are in the Father's house where the little ones can experience just what the justice and mercy of the Father can do for them. These are the rooms where only adoration, praise, and thanksgiving can exist. In these rooms exist the communion of saints. How can we not take the outstretched hand of our brothers and sisters in holiness who fill us with wonder, to bring us closer to their own rooms?

If we know how to recognize the merciful tenderness of God in our daily lives, we can also begin to write the story of our own souls, that is to say with Thérèse, "to begin to tell what will be my task for all eternity: to recount the story of God's mercies" (Ms A, 2r).

REFLECTION QUESTIONS

It is sometimes easier to identify your understanding of mercy and judgment by recalling a human relationship. Instead of thinking about God in the abstract, think about another person with whom you may be in conflict or a person that you may find difficult to love. Within that all-too-real relationship it may be possible to discover your personal truth about justice and mercy. Once your truth is discovered it should be brought to the Lord in prayer.

Consuming One's Life in Love

FOCUS POINT

Thérèse could recognize no other path on her journey than the path to be totally consumed by God. Nothing else mattered and anything else was a temptation or even a weakness. To be blessed was to live only for the Lord.

My Lord, I thank you for all the blessings you have granted me, in particular, for having me pass the stringent test of suffering. On judgment day, I will think of you carrying the scepter of the Cross. As you have judged me worthy to share this most precious Cross with you, when I am in heaven, I hope to look like you and see my body glorified with the blessed wounds of your Passion....

After being exiled on earth, I hope to go and rejoice in your presence in our Father's house. However, I do not want to gain merits just for heaven. I want to work for your divine love for the sole purpose of pleasing you, consoling your Sacred Heart, and saving souls who will love you for all eternity.

Lord, at the twilight of this life, I will appear to you with empty hands because I do not ask you to keep count of my good deeds. All of our laws are flawed in your eyes. I would like, then, to cloak myself with your law and from your love, receive you, for eternity. I want no other crown or throne than you, my Beloved....

To you, time has no meaning. A single day is like a thousand years. In a single moment, you could prepare me to appear before you....

In order to live within an act of perfect love, I offer myself in sacrifice to your merciful love, begging you to consume me endlessly, letting my soul overflow with the waves of your infinite tenderness. In this way, my Lord, may I become a martyr for your divine love....

After having prepared me to appear before you, if only this martyr could make me finally die, so that my soul could leap into the eternal embrace of your merciful love....

My Beloved, with each heartbeat, I want to infinitely renew this offering, until such a time when shadows fade and I will be able to again tell you of my love, face to face, eternally!

Thérèse of Lisieux, Pri 6

Thérèse wants to be consumed, like a log on a fire that has given all of its heat. By letting the log be destroyed by the fire, a gentle warmth settles over everyone. That is all we expect from it. This is what each of us learns by letting ourselves be endlessly consumed along the road of love, by letting our souls overflow with the waves of infinite tenderness which are locked up in the Lord.

Like the fire which needs air to burn, we also need the oxygen of love from above to be consumed in love. Just as the flame of love was given life on the Cross through the mutual love between the Father and the Son, in the same way, we need the flame of God's love to withstand the trial of suffering. Crosses are there, along the road; they are carried in proportion to our love. It is the measure of love which constitutes our strength, the strength that we receive from your love which is beyond measure.

In effect, we are called to follow: "Be imitators of God, as beloved children, and live in love, as Christ loved us and gave himself up for us, a fragrant offering and a sacrifice to God" (Eph 5:1–2). It is that we must truly live our lives in him, "rooted and built up in him and established in the faith" (Col 2:6–7). Jesus' last words, when his loving service was complete, were "it is finished" (Jn 19:30). The disciple follows the Master. As Christ did, the disciple consumes his life in love and finishes it in the glory of the resurrection.

As the Master did, he consumes it, day by day, in the confident hope of God's eternal bounty of love. Says Thérèse, "Beloved Eagle, one day, I hope you will come get your little bird and, taking it up to your hearth of love, you will immerse it for eternity in the burning abyss of that love to which it offered itself as a victim" (Ms B, 5v). We will be consumed because we will be plunged into the abyss of our Lord's love. All of the cinders of our earthly course will disappear in the fire of the Lord's love.

This is the route: always on our earthly way let ourselves be drawn toward the eternal, for Thérèse reflects: "What draws me to the heavenly homeland is the Father's call. It's the hope of finally loving him as I so wanted and the thought that I could make him loved by a multitude of souls who would bless him eternally" (LT 254). After having sought to be filled by the Spirit, how can we be alone in the kingdom of love? To love and make love, that is the norm of the little way and a life in the totality of God. To live that, in our smallness, we cry to Jesus with Thérèse: "Consume your sacrificial victim by the fire of your Divine Love" (Ms A, 84r).

One single little flame is not enough for God. If he told us: "Little children, let us love, not in word or speech, but in truth and action" (1 Jn 3:18), it is to bring about a verification of our love and not to judge the weight of our merits and deeds.

Those who search for themselves through love do not love deeply. The only love suitable for God is the dynamics of our own route. To make God happy is the expression of our true love for him, seeing that "it is more blessed to give than receive" (Acts 20:35). By living our daily life in the generosity of love, we participate in the redeeming work of our Lord whose life had been a totality of love, and in Jesus' birth for the Cross.

How do we appear before you, Lord? It would be suitable to come with full hands; full of what we will have done for you or for our brothers and sisters through you. Isn't that real proof of love? Thérèse says the contrary: "With empty hands, because I do not ask you to keep count of my good deeds" and not with hands clenched around all she would have done. Thus, we must appear with open and empty hands, so that the Lord "can put the precious gem of his love into the palms of our open hands." What, then, can we present to the Lord, if not our own gift of love which we will make grow by the power of love? We must offer God to God, with our hands opened wide, with a free heart and a burning love. Isn't this what life in heaven will be? We will contemplate, in our open hands, all of the gifts of love God gave us, in order to offer them back to him and give him eternal thanks in recognition of his love.

We walk an earthly route, entranced by Jesus, the sun of love, saying with Thérèse: "O Divine Word, you are the beloved Eagle that I adore and am drawn to! You have come down to this world of exile to suffer and die in order to lead all souls to the eternal home of the Blessed Trinity" (Ms B, 5v). If Jesus walked the Father's route toward humankind, then humankind can walk the earthly road towards the Father. We are drawn by the grace which is given to us to draw us toward that goal, the grace to see that we have received "the power to comprehend, with all the saints, what is the breadth and length and height and depth, and to know the love of Christ which surpasses knowledge" (Eph 3:18–19). We must understand to know, know to love, love in the consumption of love.

If we lose our spark along the way, is it not because we are lacking the only true desire which gives meaning to the road: the eternal meeting with love at the twilight of our life? It is easy to be bogged down and not advance, but it would be dangerous to live as if we had reached the end. Time doesn't exist in eternity. Ever since Jesus came to live among us as a man in our world, he has revealed its seriousness. Let us not waste time! Let the desire to see God and share his communion of love dwell in us always.

> I have only one desire, it is to see you, my Lord.
> I want nothing more than to die for your love.
> I want to die to begin to live.
> I want to die to unite myself with Jesus.
> *Thérèse of Lisieux, RP 3, 20v–21r*

The mortal body must be destroyed so that we may enter into the eternal face to face of love with God, a never-ending joy. The only desire which has any worth to push us along the road is the desire to love until we die of love, until we are completely consumed by love.

We are not consumed bit by bit like an organism that sees its strength gradually wane. That experience is really a form of martyrdom. It is a martyrdom of love when the being is totally consumed by itself and imbued with eternal love, the merciful love of the Lord which forces us to explode from love. This only happens at the end time. But from time to time, we may see bits of it through renewed sparks of love and offering, by welcoming the many loving favors given to us by God. But the only favor, in Thérèse's estimation, is to have "interludes of Divine Love" in our lives (Ms C, 8v), when all the earth would be assumed by love and consumed in love. Then the eternal day of God will open itself to us, a day of never-ending light where we can repeat our love to God, eternally and face to face. And in thanksgiving for the earthly route accomplished, we could only say with Thérèse: "I do not regret having given myself to love" (DE 30.9).

REFLECTION QUESTIONS

The Little Way seems to be a way that is much more difficult than what might first be imagined. Every choice, every desire, every impulse must be chosen and acted upon only because it gives glory and honor to God. It is an all-consuming way, a way that bends, molds, and finally shapes a person into a beautiful vessel that is pleasing to the Lord. What needs to be bended, molded, and finally shaped in you in order to pray, "I do not regret having given myself to love"?

Bibliography

TO DISCOVER MORE about Saint Thérèse of Lisieux, the following books are suggested.

Baudouin-Croix, Marie. *Léonie Martin: A Difficult Life.* Dublin: Veritas, 1993.

Beevers, John. *Saint Thérèse, the Little Flower: The Making of a Saint.* Reprint edition. Rockford, IL: TAN Books and publishers, 1976.

Chalon, Jean. *Thérèse of Lisieux: A Life of Love.* Liguori, MO: Liguori Publications, 1997.

Clarke, John, translator. Vols. I and II. *St. Thérèse of Lisieux: General Correspondence.* Washington, D.C.: ICS Publications, 1996.

Clarke, John, translator. *St. Thérèse of Lisieux: Her Last Conversations.* Washington, D.C.: ICS Publications, 1977.

Clarke, John, translator. *Story of a Soul.* 3rd edition. Washington, D.C.: ICS Publications, 1996.

Emert, Joyce. *Louis Martin: Father of a Saint.* Staten Island, NY: Alba House, 1983.

Guitton, Jean. *The Spiritual Genius of Saint Thérèse of Lisieux.* Liguori, MO: Liguori/Triumph, 1997.

Kinney, Donald, translator. *The Poetry of St. Thérèse of Lisieux.* Washington, D.C.: ICS Publications, 1996.

Nelson, John. *The Little Way of Saint Thérèse of Lisieux.* Liguori, MO: Liguori Publications, 1997.

O'Mahony, Christopher, editor. *St. Thérèse of Lisieux by Those Who Knew Her.* Dublin: Veritas Publications, 1975. Reprint 1988.

Piat, O.F.M., Stéphane-Joseph. *The Story of a Family: The Home of the Little Flower.* Translated by a Benedictine of Stanbrook Abbey. Reprint edition. Rockford, IL: TAN Publications, 1995.

Piat, O.F.M., Stéphane-Joseph. *Céline: Sister Geneviève of the Holy Face.* Translated by the Carmelite Sisters of Eucharist of Colchester, Connecticut from the second edition, 1964. San Francisco: Ignatius Press, 1997.

Tonnelier, Constant. *Through the Year With Saint Thérèse of Lisieux: Living the Little Way.* Liguori, MO: Liguori Publications, 1998.

Wust, Louis and Marjorie. *Zélie Martin: Mother of St. Thérèse.* Boston: St. Paul Editions, 1969.